AIMR Conference Proceedings
Equity Trading: Execution and Analysis

Proceedings of the AIMR seminar "Equity Trading: The Next Revolution"

24–25 March 2003
Chicago

Harold S. Bradley
Minder Cheng
Jennifer Conrad
Lawrence E. Harris
Marcus Hooper

Marie S. Konstance, CFA
Richard G. Leibovitch
Robert A. Schwartz
Benn Steil, *moderator*
Wayne H. Wagner

Association for Investment Management and Research

Dedicated to the Highest Standards of Ethics, Education, and Professional Practice in Investment Management and Research.

This proceedings qualifies for credit under the guidelines of the Professional Development Program. Using Reference Time, this proceedings qualifies for 6 credit hours. The self-test for this proceedings can be found at www.aimr.org/pdprogram/self-tests_list.html. For more information on the PD Program (including how to use Clock Time and the Standard Documentation in lieu of the self-test), go to www.aimr.org/pdprogram.

CFA®, Chartered Financial Analyst®, AIMR-PPS®, GIPS®, and Financial Analysts Journal® are just a few of the trademarks owned by the Association for Investment Management and Research®. To view a list of the Association for Investment Management and Research's trademarks and the Guide for Use of AIMR's Marks, please visit our website at www.aimr.org.

©2003, Association for Investment Management and Research

All rights reserved. No part of this publication may be reproduced, stored in a retrieval system, or transmitted, in any form or by any means, electronic, mechanical, photocopying, recording, or otherwise, without prior written permission of the copyright holder.

**AIMR CONFERENCE PROCEEDINGS
(USPS 013-739 ISSN 1535-0207) 2003**

Is published four times a year in March, April, July, and December, by the Association for Investment Management and Research at 560 Ray C. Hunt Drive, Charlottesville, VA. **Periodical postage paid at Charlottesville, Virginia, and additional mailing offices.**

This publication is designed to provide accurate and authoritative information with regard to the subject matter covered. It is sold with the understanding that the publisher is not engaged in rendering legal, accounting, or other professional services. If legal advice or other expert assistance is required, the services of a competent professional should be sought.

Copies are mailed as a benefit of membership to CFA® charterholders. Subscriptions also are available at $100.00 USA. For one year. Address all circulation communications to AIMR Conference Proceedings, 560 Ray C. Hunt Drive, Charlottesville, Virginia 22903, USA; Phone 434-951-5499; Fax 434-951-5262. For change of address. Send mailing label and new address six weeks in advance.

Postmaster: Please send address changes to AIMR Conference Proceedings, Association for Investment Management and Research, P.O. Box 3668, Charlottesville, Virginia 22903.

ISBN 1-932495-04-5
Printed in the United States of America
September 12, 2003

Editorial Staff
Kathryn Dixon Jost, CFA
Editor

Maryann Dupes *Book Editor*	Jaynee M. Dudley *Production Manager*
Sophia E. Battaglia *Assistant Editor*	Rebecca L. Bowman *Assistant Editor*
Kelly T. Bruton/Lois A. Carrier *Composition and Production*	Kara H. Morris *Online Production*

Contents

Authors	v
Overview Ann C. Logue, CFA	1

Institutional Trading Costs and Trading Systems
    Jennifer Conrad
    Kevin M. Johnson
    Sunil Wahal
	3

Trading Cost Analysis and Management Marie S. Konstance, CFA	8
Institutional Order Flow and the Hurdles to Superior Performance Wayne H. Wagner	13
Pretrade Cost Analysis and Management of Implementation Shortfall Minder Cheng	26
Views of an "Informed" Trader Harold S. Bradley	35
Cost versus Liquidity: The Quest for Best Execution Wayne H. Wagner	45
The Impact of the Myners Report on Global Investors Marcus Hooper	52
Market Microstructure and the Regulation of Markets Lawrence E. Harris	60

Focus on Equity

www.aimr.org/featuring/ed_central/

Following is a sample of the wealth of information on Equity found in the Education Central area of AIMR's website.

Featured AIMR Publications
www.aimr**pubs**.org

Equity Valuation in a Global Context
(AIMR Conference Proceedings, 2003)

Closing the Gap between Financial Reporting and Reality
(AIMR Conference Proceedings, 2003)

Featured Webcasts
www.aimrdirect.org

The Future of Investment Management
Highlights from the 2003 AIMR Annual Conference
Peter L. Bernstein, Richard C. Breeden, James E. Heard, Robert C. Merton, Meir Statman, and Robert G. Zielinski, CFA
(May 2003)

Fusion Investing: Integrating Behavioral Finance and Fundamental Analysis
Charles M.C. Lee
(July 2003)

Loose Ends in Valuation: Eliminating the Bias
Aswath Damodaran
(January 2003)

Featured AIMR Conferences
www.aimr.org/conferences

Equity Research and Valuation Techniques
2–3 December 2003
Philadelphia, PA, USA

Authors

We would like to thank Benn Steil for serving as moderator at this conference and Ann Logue, CFA, for being the guest content editor and for writing the overview for this proceedings. We also wish to express our sincere gratitude to the authors listed below for their contributions to both the conference and this proceedings:

Harold S. Bradley is senior vice president of American Century Investment Management, where he leads the Investment Ideas and Incubation Group and serves as a member of the company's Strategic Planning Group and Investment Oversight Committee. Previously, he served as a member of the Kansas City Board of Trade and as marketing director of the exchange. Mr. Bradley has testified in front of the U.S. Congress on behalf of customer-oriented market reforms, including limit-order display rules and complete disclosure of investment advisor soft-dollar practices. He is a graduate of Marquette University.

Minder Cheng is global head of equity and currency trading at Barclays Global Investors, where he oversees equity and currency trading activities worldwide and heads the firm's trading research effort. Previously, he served as executive director of proprietary trading at Sumitomo Finance International and as vice president of proprietary trading at Salomon Brothers. Dr. Cheng also managed several projects for the Research and Planning Division of the NYSE. He holds a B.A. from National Taiwan University and an M.B.A. and a Ph.D. from the University of California at Berkeley.

Jennifer Conrad is McMichael Distinguished Professor of Finance at the Kenan-Flagler Business School at the University of North Carolina at Chapel Hill. Her current research focuses on the ability of asset-pricing models to explain predictable patterns in returns. Professor Conrad has won two teaching awards and serves as associate editor of the *Journal of Finance, Journal of Financial Research,* and *Journal of Financial and Quantitative Analysis*. She holds a B.S. from Butler University and an M.B.A. and a Ph.D. from the University of Chicago.

Lawrence E. Harris holds the Fred V. Keenan Chair in Finance at the Marshall School of Business at the University of Southern California. He is currently on assignment to the U.S. SEC, where he serves as chief economist and director of the Office of Economic Analysis. Professor Harris has written extensively on exchange trading rules, volatility, stock index markets, and market regulation, and is a consultant for traders, exchanges, investment banks, and regulators. He is the author of *Trading and Exchanges: Market Microstructure for Practitioners*. Professor Harris holds a Ph.D. from the University of Chicago.

Marcus Hooper is managing director at Duvacy Ltd. Previously, he served in the investment management divisions of HBOS, Dresdner, and AXA. Mr. Hooper has assisted in the development and direction of various projects carried out by the Investment Managers Association, British Banking Association, European Commission, and London Stock Exchange. Additionally, he has authored papers on financial market behavior, including best execution, alternative trading systems, and transaction analysis. Mr. Hooper is a regular speaker at industry conferences and has lectured executive M.B.A. classes on financial topics.

Kevin M. Johnson is a principal, director of research, and portfolio manager at Aronson+Johnson+Ortiz, LP. Previously, he served as a portfolio manager in DuPont's internal pension group and as director of core management at The Vanguard Group. Dr. Johnson holds a B.S. in finance and economics from the University of Delaware and a Ph.D. from the University of North Carolina.

Marie S. Konstance, CFA, is senior vice president and manager of analytical product sales at Investment Technology Group, Inc., which supplies a wide range of research tools, including pre- and post-trade transaction cost analysis, optimization software, and risk modeling. Previously, she managed the Analytical Valuation Services Group at Morgan Stanley and marketed derivatives products at First Boston Corporation. Ms. Konstance holds a B.A. from Colgate University and an M.B.A. from Harvard University.

Benn Steil is the André Meyer Senior Fellow in International Economics at the Council on Foreign Relations. He serves as a consultant and analyst for investment banks, securities exchanges, and government bodies around the world. Dr. Steil is the editor of *International Finance* and the author of several books, including *Institutional Investors* and *The European Equity Markets*. He holds a B.S. from the Wharton School at the University of Pennsylvania and an M.Phil. and a D.Phil. from Oxford University.

Wayne H. Wagner is co-founder and chairman of the Plexus Group, which provides implementation evaluation and advisory services to U.S. and global money managers, brokerage firms, and pension plan sponsors. Previously, he served as a founding partner of Wilshire Associates and as chief investment officer of Wilshire Asset Management. Mr. Wagner has written and spoken frequently on many trading and investing subjects and has received two Graham and Dodd Awards of Excellence from the *Financial Analysts Journal*. He is author and editor of *The Complete Guide to Securities Transactions: Improving Performance and Reducing Costs* and co-author of *MILLIONAIRE: The Simplest Explanation of How an Index Fund Can Turn Your Lunch Money into a Fortune*. Mr. Wagner holds a B.B.A. from the University of Wisconsin and an M.S. from Stanford University.

Sunil Wahal is associate professor of finance at Goizueta Business School at Emory University. His research focuses on the behavior and impact of institutional investors on capital markets. Professor Wahal has authored papers on subjects ranging from institutional shareholder activism to the cost of soft-dollar trading by institutions. He is the recipient of the Emory Williams Teaching Award. Professor Wahal holds a Ph.D. from the University of North Carolina at Chapel Hill.

Overview

Ann C. Logue, CFA
Freelance Communications
Chicago

When market returns are down across the board, trading costs—never insignificant—become a vital factor in generating portfolio returns. Recent activities, including the release of AIMR's Trade Management Guidelines and the study "Institutional Investment in the United Kingdom" (commonly called the "Myners Report"), have forced money management firms to consider transaction costs in light of their fiduciary responsibility, not just their performance targets.

The problem is that many transaction costs are hidden. The obvious explicit costs are commission, spread, and market impact, which can be discovered without much effort. But costs such as delay, missed trades, and other opportunity costs are larger than the explicit costs and can have a substantial negative effect on portfolio performance. Unfortunately, these implicit costs cannot readily be measured, and complicating matters further, many commonly used techniques for measuring transactions costs are subject to gaming by traders. Consequently, investment management firms must not only understand the various types of transaction costs and how best to measure them but also be able to explain the intricacies of different cost measurement systems to the clients who use them.

The authors in this proceedings give differing perspectives on the magnitude of the problem and offer techniques for managing costs before, during, and after the trade. They pay particular attention to the management of opportunity costs relative to the management of the trading desk and emphasize the need for getting portfolio managers to address trading costs at the point of idea generation and for preventing traders from destroying portfolio value in lieu of maximizing their bonuses.

Trading Cost Analysis

Jennifer Conrad, Kevin Johnson, and Sunil Wahal explain that trading costs can be a significant drag on portfolio performance. Thus, investors should be looking for ways to minimize these costs. One such way is to use alternative trading systems, such as electronic communications networks and crossing systems. A study comparing the trading costs on alternative trading systems with the costs of using traditional brokers generally reveals lower costs on the alternative trading systems.

Marie Konstance explains that analyzing trading costs is difficult, but anything that can be done to lower them goes straight to the bottom line. This cost-reduction process begins with effective measurement and then moves on to analysis and finally to control. Even if traders cannot control all factors affecting trading costs, small improvements can lead to a big impact on overall costs and performance.

Institutional investors trade in the same markets as retail investors, says Wayne Wagner, but typically, institutional investors work with much larger amounts of dollars and shares. These large trades do not appear to be cost-effective when viewed from various perspectives, which raises the question: Is trading cost related to liquidity demand or to market frictions?

Minder Cheng presents a format for managing trading costs before the trade takes place. Measuring trading costs entails looking at six components: commission, bid–ask spread, market trend, liquidity impact, opportunity cost, and slippage. These components combine to determine the implementation shortfall. But trade cost management requires more than just measuring completed trade costs; it requires forecasting the costs of future trades and then incorporating the forecasts into trade list generation and portfolio optimization. By measuring, forecasting, and managing trading costs, a firm can work toward the ultimate goal—best execution.

Standards

The U.S. SEC and industry standard setters, such as AIMR, are likely to keep the pressure on firms to increase trade transparency and improve record keeping and accountability for trading activity, argues Harold Bradley. To avoid problems, firms will need to be proactive in investing in new technologies, and in the process, they should thoroughly scrutinize their commissions, brokerage rates, and order execution process; establish a consistent method to measure best execution; and above all, let their traders be traders. To meet these challenges, Bradley advocates wider use of electronic communications networks, which offer greater equality and efficiency and thus can help firms significantly reduce trading costs while better serving clients.

Wayne Wagner discusses the trade-offs between cost and liquidity. Trading is a process that extends from the portfolio manager to the trader. The trader, however, often faces a dilemma: cost or liquidity. The answer to this riddle is part of the larger issue of best execution, which has been addressed by many organizations—from the U.S. SEC to AIMR. AIMR's Trade Management Guidelines get best execution right, in principle, but Wagner believes the guidelines fall short in other areas.

Regulatory Perspective

Finally, this proceedings has observations from a regulatory perspective. The British government commissioned a review of trading costs and other distortions in the institutional investment process, especially as they affected pension fund returns. The resulting study, commonly known as the "Myners Report," recommends more disclosure from institutional money managers, which has led to an increased focus on transaction costs. Marcus Hooper discusses how this report affects global investors.

Lawrence Harris talks about regulation from the perspective of the market's microstructure. The current market structure has price inefficiencies, particularly from access fees, market data revenue and rebates, and the use of volume-weighted average price as a trading benchmark. These inefficiencies have negative effects on price transparency, best execution practices, and market competition. Luckily, ways may exist to improve market efficiency without resorting to changes in regulation.

Conclusion

If a trading desk is adding value to a portfolio, then it may be able to justify its trading costs. But if its trading practices are hurting the performance of clients' portfolios, then changes have to be made to lower trading costs. Only through a detailed analysis of trading costs can a firm assess where its traders are helping clients (and where they are not). Because any trading costs that can be eliminated immediately will increase the bottom line, firms must keep tabs on these costs. And although cost control is important in every market environment, it takes on a particular urgency in the current bear market.

Institutional Trading Costs and Trading Systems

Jennifer Conrad
McMichael Distinguished Professor of Finance
University of North Carolina at Chapel Hill
Chapel Hill, North Carolina

Kevin M. Johnson
Principal
Aronson+Johnson+Ortiz, LP
Philadelphia

Sunil Wahal
Associate Professor of Finance
Emory University
Atlanta

> Trading costs can be a significant drag on portfolio performance. One way to minimize trading costs is to use alternative trading systems, such as electronic communications networks and crossing systems. In a study comparing the trading costs on alternative trading systems with the costs of using traditional brokers, the data reveal generally lower costs on the alternative trading systems.

Financial institutions have a number of opportunities to optimize their trading efficiencies and reduce costs. They can break up trades into smaller pieces, or they can use better traders or brokers, which means they will have to take into account whether to use soft-dollar brokers or research brokers. Institutions can also be more patient; that is, they can wait longer to execute the trades. By waiting to execute, however, institutions run the risk of not filling part of a trade, which raises the issue of opportunity costs. Another option is for institutions to use limit orders, a less-aggressive trading strategy than market orders. Institutions can also use alternative trading systems, which is the strategy discussed in this presentation.

Editor's note: This presentation is based on the article "Institutional Trading and Alternative Trading Systems" by Jennifer Conrad, Kevin M. Johnson, and Sunil Wahal (*Journal of Financial Economics*, forthcoming). This material was presented at the preconference workshop solely by Jennifer Conrad. The joint question and answer session for this presentation follows Wayne Wagner's presentation.

This presentation reports the findings of a study that examined the effect that two types of trading systems have on financial institutions' implementation shortfall execution costs. In this case, the two trading systems examined were crossing systems and electronic communications networks (ECNs), which were compared with a benchmark of broker-filled orders.

Establishing the Parameters

To examine the costs involved in institutional trading and to compare these costs across alternative trading systems, Kevin Johnson, Sunil Wahal, and I separated total execution costs into implicit costs (or market impact costs) and explicit costs (or commissions). We compared the magnitude of these costs relative to the decision price. For the entire order, we defined decision price as the closing price on the day before the first trade hit the market, even for the multiple-mechanism piece of an order.

Previous studies by Donald Keim at the Wharton School at the University of Pennsylvania, Ananth

Madhavan at Investment Technology Group (ITG), and Lewis Chan and Joseph Lakonishok at the University of Illinois have indicated that implicit costs average approximately 60–80 bps and explicit costs average 20–30 bps per trade.[1] Furthermore, costs across orders, across stocks, and even across traders vary, which raises many issues when attempting to measure such costs. For example, when examining samples, researchers must decide how to include the delay in filling an order and how to account for the unfilled portion of the order.

For this particular set of data, my colleagues and I dealt with the unfilled pieces of an order by using the closing price 10 days out and imputing from that number a market impact for the unfilled piece of the order. Whether we closed the books 10, 15, or 21 days out, little difference was apparent in the sample.

Crossing Systems. We used two different types of crossing systems in our sample—ITG POSIT and Instinet Crossing—and no NYSE crossing sessions. By far the largest part of our sample came from ITG POSIT; Instinet Crossing, which is an after-hours crossing system, accounted for only about 4,000 orders in a total sample of close to 800,000. Furthermore, we segregated the samples from the two systems because they trade in different types of circumstances. These crossing systems use the underlying market to generate the price; consequently, there was no price discovery in this sample and no market impact by definition.

ECNs. For the purposes of our sample, which ran from 1996 to 1998, the only ECN available for institutional investors was Instinet. Bloomberg appeared during the last quarter of 1998, which put it outside our time frame.

ECNs have two features of particular interest. One is that they provide anonymity. Another is that they provide price discovery, which indicated to us that they are active market participants. In fact, a paper written by Roger Huang shows that ECNs provide the bulk of price discovery in 8 out of the 10 most active stocks and in 12 out of the 30 most active stocks on Nasdaq.[2]

The data sample, which we received from Plexus Group (thanks to Wayne Wagner), included the umbrella order in the particular stocks that we examined. We were able to obtain the following information for each trade:

- security identification,
- indicator of whether the transaction was a buy or a sell order,
- trade prices,
- trade dates,
- order instruction (i.e., whether it was a market, limit, or crossed order),
- style classifications of the institutions, and
- broker identification.

The broker identification indicated the particular trading system to which each order was sent. In addition, although we did not have the name of the institutional investor, we were often able to determine the investing style of the institution—that is, whether it was a diversified, momentum, or value trader.

We also obtained the security-day volume from Instinet's day system. This information was useful because we were testing whether there were significant differences in average trade costs across these various systems. Typically, we assumed that if investors were behaving optimally, average excess costs would be zero; that is, the data would demonstrate a state of equilibrium. If average excess costs were not zero, we wanted to know why disequilibrium existed. Were our data derived from a period of temporary disequilibrium? Were things changing during our sample period? Were the data moving toward equilibrium? Had we missed something in our measures of excess costs?

Finally, because of two changes in the regulatory environment during our sample period—the change in the order handling rules and the change in the tick size, both in 1997—we were interested in measuring changes to Instinet's market share over time.

Description of the Data and Analysis

We looked at 59 anonymous institutions over nine quarters, from the first quarter of 1996 to the first quarter of 1998. The sample consisted of 797,068 orders broken into 2.15 million trades that were valued at about $1.6 trillion. Most of our analysis focused on execution costs at the level of the order, but later in the analysis, we examined costs at the level of the trade. As it turned out, some of the orders in our sample had trades sent to multiple trading mechanisms. For example, one trade went to a crossing system and another to an ECN. Therefore, we classified orders as either single- or multiple-mechanism orders.

---

[1] Donald Keim and Ananth Madhavan, "Anatomy of the Trading Process: Empirical Evidence on the Behavior of Institutional Traders," *Journal of Financial Economics* (March 1995):371–398; Lewis Chan and Joseph Lakonishok, "The Behavior of Stock Prices around Institutional Trades," *Journal of Finance* (September 1995):1147–74.

[2] Roger Huang, "The Quality of ECN and Nasdaq Market Maker Quotes," *Journal of Finance* (June 2002):1285–1319.

About 91 percent of the sampled orders were single-mechanism orders; the remaining 9 percent involved multiple trading systems. Yet, these multiple-mechanism orders represented about 47.5 percent of the sample's total volume in orders, so they certainly needed to be included in our analysis. We addressed them separately.

We first ranked orders according to their level of difficulty, as measured by dollar amount. The multiple-mechanism orders, averaging about $2 million per order, proved to be the most difficult in our sample. The next most difficult were broker-filled orders, at about $1.4 million per order. ECN orders averaged about $194,000, and crossing system orders averaged about $180,000. Based on these differences, when we compared execution costs across these different trading systems, we wanted to control for the differences in the order characteristics that were associated with the different platforms.

Not surprisingly, more difficult orders took longer. We observed an average of about four trades per multiple-mechanism order, about 2.2 trades per broker-filled order, and about 1.5 trades per order in the two alternative trading system mechanisms. We also observed a corresponding difference in the fill rate—the more difficult the trade, the lower the fill rate.

Simple Matching Analysis. The first step was a simple match, which was probably the most intuitive but also the least rigorous analysis. The ideal situation would have been for a manager to evenly divide an order into two trades of the same size on the same day and send them to two different trading mechanisms. It would then be a simple task to compare the costs of the two trades, measure the difference between the two costs, and determine which, if either, was cheaper.

Unfortunately, data that straightforward were not available. We tried, however, to find the closest comparisons that we could in the data that we had. For example, instead of defining a comparable trade as being exactly the same stock, we defined a comparable trade as being of the same type of stock, having similar size, and occurring as close to the same time as possible. Then we measured the difference between the trading costs for broker-filled orders and the trading costs for orders filled on the alternative trading systems.

We used a number of dummy variables for matching purposes. We were able to match perfectly on three of these variables: exchange listing, order instruction, and whether it was a buy or sell order. (Everyone seems to find significant differences in execution costs across buys and sells.) We also matched within a tolerance of ±10 percent on two other control variables that we think constitute an important indicator of the difficulty of an order: (1) the market cap of the stock being traded and (2) the size of the order relative to the average daily volume over the five days preceding the order. This average volume was calculated as the geometric mean of the volume over the five days preceding the order.

Using this methodology, we were able to match about 99 percent of our crossed orders and about 90 percent of our ECN orders. We had multiple matches most of the time, so we could take an average of the matches to get a fairly precise measured difference. We found that the crossing system orders in our sample were 30 bps cheaper to execute than broker-filled orders; ECN orders were 66 bps cheaper, on average, than broker-filled orders.

Although such differences are significant, they are only valid to the extent that the matching is valid. Consequently, we verified the findings by using even more restrictive matching algorithms. We examined pricing in the ECN system, in the crossing system, and among broker-filled orders to determine if those factors explained the cost difference, but they did not. We then looked for differences through time by restricting the match within a quarter. Again, there was no difference. Finally, we applied the most restrictive matching algorithm available to us. Specifically, we required a match on the same stock within the same week. This requirement caused the number of orders that we successfully matched to drop precipitously. We matched about one-half of our crossed orders and about one-third of our ECN orders. Only the most liquid and the largest market-capitalization-weighted stocks matched those stocks at the 97th percentile of market capitalization on the crossed orders and those stocks at the 99th percentile on ECN orders. We did not expect any differential to persist in such liquid stocks, but it did. Crossed orders in that sample were 9 bps cheaper than broker-filled orders, whereas ECN orders were 6 bps cheaper. Overall, no matter how restrictive the matching algorithm, the differential remained fairly robust.

Regression-Matching Specification Analysis. Previous studies, such as those of Keim and Madhavan mentioned earlier, have shown that significant differences exist among institutions' abilities to manage trades efficiently. Unfortunately, we could not match based on specific financial institutions. Therefore, we switched to a different regression methodology that simulated the differences between financial institutions by using dummy variables for crossing systems and ECNs. The results are shown in **Table 1**.

Table 1. Execution Cost Differences Based on Regression

System	Data Type	Buy	Sell
Crosses	Trading System	–31 bps	–32 bps
	Institution	–17	–14
ECNs	Trading System	–28	–66
	Institution	–28	–54

Table 2. Execution Cost Differences Based on Selectivity Regressions

System	Data Type	Buy	Sell
Crosses	Trading System	–55 bps	–66 bps
	Institution	–16	+31
ECNs	Trading System	–62	–68
	Institution	–26	–45

The first row for each system presents the execution cost differential without including institution-specific dummy variables, and the second row shows the differential from a regression specification that included a dummy variable for each of the 59 financial institutions. The result is a more conservative execution cost differential because it accounts for the behavior of each institution. For example, in this specification, an institution that sent most of its trades to a crossing system and also had lower execution costs would have those lower execution costs ascribed to the institution rather than the crossing system. With or without the institution-specific dummy variable, however, the differentials were still negative. The alternative trading system in each of these cases seemed to generate lower execution costs. Without the dummy variable, the magnitudes of the differentials in the regression analysis were comparable with the magnitudes in the matching analysis. That is, the crossing systems were about 30 bps cheaper per trade without institution-specific variables, and the ECNs were 30–70 bps cheaper. When we allowed for institution-specific characteristics, the differentials were smaller but still negative and economically significant.

Endogenous Switching Regression Analysis. Whether we used simple matching analysis or regression-matching specification analysis, both alternative trading systems proved to be less costly than broker-filled orders. But we still wondered if we missed something. I mentioned earlier that the broker-filled orders were more difficult, so we decided to take that difficulty into account in another way. We used an endogenous switching regression, which is a technique that has been used to examine whether the execution cost differences for upstairs orders on the NYSE are related to the higher degree of difficulty of those orders. If the level of difficulty of an order is what determines which trading system is used, this type of regression will allow us to see the effect by removing that factor from the equation.

The results of the switching regression analysis, shown in **Table 2**, indicate that, except for sell orders sent to crossing systems, all the differentials were negative, which means the alternative trading systems generate slightly lower execution costs, even when taking order difficulty into account in this way. Because the differentials were consistently negative, these results are fairly robust.

Multiple-Mechanism Orders

The analyses I have described so far were based on single-mechanism orders—those that generated trades on only one system. Such orders represented only about one-half of the volume in our sample. The other half of the volume consisted of multiple-mechanism orders. We asked the same question with these orders: What are the execution cost differentials across these different trading systems? This time, however, we examined the data at the trade level rather than the order level. Once again we used regression methodology, but we also included variables that allowed such conditions as the position of the trade in the order, the execution costs up to that point in the order, and the number of switches between trading platforms during the course of the order to affect the estimated execution cost differential.

We found that execution costs for the two alternative trading systems remained lower than broker-filled costs, with the crossing system 8 bps lower for buys and 6 bps lower for sells. ECNs were about 21 bps lower for buys and 23 bps lower for sells. We also looked for evidence that brokers were being used as dealers of last resort, called in to handle the last, and possibly the most difficult, piece of a trade.

We did see a small increase in the propensity to use brokers in the last part of the trade. Throughout the sample, brokers were used for about 50 percent of all trades and about 60 percent of the last trades in the orders, which means that a full 40 percent of the last trades were filled by an alternative trading system. We did find some evidence in the regressions that when a broker was the last trading mechanism in an order, the execution was more costly. That is, we found about a 14 bp increase in the cost of the last trade if it was filled by a broker, but only for buys and not for sells. The data were not particularly robust across different specifications. In other words, the analysis shows weak evidence that brokers are the dealers of last resort, being given the most difficult piece of a trade.

Observations

If institutional investors are trying hard to minimize the costs of trading, then why do the differential costs that we observed in the study persist? Although the differentials were observable at every point of the analysis, we did find evidence that they declined during the time period from which the sample was taken. The two regulatory changes mentioned earlier—the change in the order handling rules and the change in tick size—coincided with the midpoint of our sample. Both changes affected the ECN part of the sample and were evidenced by a decline in the tendency to use ECNs, a decline in Instinet's market share, and a decline in the differential execution cost. Even so, an economically significant differential persisted at the end of the sample. Because the crossing systems we examined were not affected by regulatory changes, their portion of the sample showed no decline in the differential.

We asked ourselves what might be causing that continued differential. We conjectured that the fill rates in our samples were biased upward for some reason. That is, if a financial institution in the sample used a crossing system to fill an order but was unsuccessful, the order would not be recorded and this lack of recording would generate an upward bias in the fill rates. Because institutions may not get their orders filled with an alternative trading system, this is an important area for future research.

Conclusions and Continuing Work

All in all, financial institutions appear to have numerous opportunities to increase their trading efficiencies and reduce their trading costs. Although we used a variety of methods to measure cost differentials in the data, the evidence indicates that large differences in excess execution costs exist between orders using alternative trading systems (ECNs and crossing systems) and broker-filled orders. We also found that the differences declined over our sample period. We were left with questions about opportunity costs—those of not trading or not filling a trade.

My colleagues and I are now developing another research project to examine the issue of opportunity costs. In particular, we are examining the costs of delaying or not filling an order. Unfortunately, these costs are associated with pieces of the order that are largely hidden, so data will be hard to find. To overcome this problem, we are using simulation to show prices moving randomly because of trading. Ultimately, we are trying to simulate how traders behave when they see random fluctuations in price (i.e., whether they are trying to take advantage of favorable movements in price and are staying out of the market when price movements are not favorable). To do this analysis, we are simulating the degree of a trader's aggressiveness during the course of the trading, which means we are establishing boundary prices to represent the maximum amounts traders are willing to pay. Beyond the boundary price, we are assuming that the trader will not trade. As a further guide for the simulation, we have established the following trading rules: trade as much as possible up to the boundary price, and fill the order as quickly as possible.

We are calibrating the model using data given to us, once again, by Plexus Group for calendar year 2000. We are using three order sizes—1 percent, 10 percent, and 100 percent of average daily volume. We are considering three alphas or boundary prices for each stock based on the volatility of the individual stock, which means we are using real data for that part of the study. We are following 4,500 stocks and doing 500 simulations of the price path for each individual stock. We have about 20 million orders, and we are allowing for 100 different periods over which a trader can decide whether to trade and how much to trade. At time period 100, we close the books.

Based on our analysis so far, we have found that fill rates for small orders are close to 100 percent, but for large orders, fill rates are closer to 80 percent. For the piece of an order that is not filled by time period 100, we have observed opportunity costs of about 3 percent, which would significantly increase the trading costs of the whole order if it were incorporated into the order execution costs. Our conclusion for this sample, therefore, is that institutions pay a steep price for not trading.

As part of our continuing efforts to understand these costs, we are trying to establish benchmarks. We are also trying to use real data on package bids to determine if our trading cost measure is consistent with a particular institutional investor's decision about whether or not to accept bids.

Trading Cost Analysis and Management

Marie S. Konstance, CFA
Senior Vice President and Manager of Analytical Product Sales
Investment Technology Group, Inc.
New York City

> Analyzing trading costs is difficult, but anything that can be done to improve them goes straight to the bottom line. This cost-reduction process begins with effective measurement and then moves on to analysis and, finally, to control. Even if traders cannot control all factors affecting trading costs, small improvements can lead to a big impact on overall costs and performance.

When the subject of transaction costs comes up, one question is often asked: "Why bother? Particularly when the markets are choppy and illiquid, and the trend is going against you, control over transaction costs is minimal. Many traders do not even have discretion over trading costs because they are acting on the instructions of the portfolio manager. Neither are the data used in trade cost analysis perfect." Although these arguments have some merit, it is also true that any reduction in transaction costs goes right to the bottom line. In this presentation, I will address why transaction cost analysis is important, how transaction cost analysis is done, and what can be learned from the process.

Academics have found that transaction costs drop significantly by using transaction cost analysis tools. Donald Keim looked at Dimensional Fund Advisors' 9–10 Small Company Fund, a standard small-cap index fund that outperformed its competitors over a 15-year period. Keim found that in recent years, informal investment rules concerning the investment universe added 72 bps to outperformance, whereas the trading strategy itself added 204 bps.[1] In other words, the transaction cost improvements contributed to the fund's outperformance.

Deciding to perform trade cost analysis is the first step. The next step is determining how to do it so that the results are meaningful. If done well, transaction cost analysis can be used to (1) meaningfully alter the trading strategy and improve trading performance and (2) refine the investment strategy.

Successful implementation is composed of three elements. The first element is measurement. A process has to be established, and it has to take place while the trade is still fresh in everyone's mind, which is important for the second element, analysis. The focus has to be on implicit, controllable costs as measured against a practical, informative benchmark. The third element is control so that hidden costs can be reduced.

Measurement

Trades can be benchmarked using one of two basic paradigms. The first is implementation shortfall, which takes a market price at a specific point in time (usually the time the order appeared on the trader's desk) and adjusts it by expected costs. The second paradigm is volume-weighted average price (VWAP). These benchmarks can give different messages, particularly in trending markets; thus, knowing the pitfalls and subtleties of each method is important. Some traders prefer VWAP because they trade in large size or they are instructed to trade as a percent of VWAP. Multiday VWAP measures are more meaningful nowadays than full-day calculations, but it can be difficult to determine when the trading period begins and ends. Is multiday measured from the start of the order to the end of the order? Or is it measured from the start of the order to the end of the last trading day to capture all of the available liquidity? The decision makes a difference in the results.

Editor's note: This presentation was given at the preconference workshop. The joint question and answer session for this presentation follows Wayne Wagner's presentation.

[1] Donald B. Keim, "An Analysis of Mutual Fund Design: The Case of Investing in Small-Cap Stocks," *Journal of Financial Economics* (February 1999):173–194.

The difference between implementation shortfall and VWAP can be seen in the following example. Suppose an order was placed to buy Prudential Financial shares on the London Stock Exchange (LSE). The order size constituted 10.5 percent of Prudential's average daily volume on the LSE. Prudential is a highly volatile issue; 21-day volatility was 446 bps. The trade was executed over three days. When the order was first placed, the price was 545.5 pence, as shown in **Figure 1**. The first execution was a little lower than that at roughly 539 pence, as shown in **Table 1**. Other pieces of the trade were executed over the next two days, after the stock's price had spiked. On a decision-price implementation shortfall basis, the cost is high—541 bps. But on a VWAP basis, the cost is only 30 bps.

VWAP smoothes out market moves. To beat VWAP, a trader just has to keep trading; eventually, the trader will look good, even if the alpha in the trade is lost. The ITG Agency Cost Estimator (ITG ACE) model of predicted costs shows that this trade should have cost 54 bps and could have been completed in half a day.

Proper trading cost measurement requires quality input, starting with regular data submission that allows tracking of the full trade execution history. Without a full execution history and trading process, the real source of the costs may be hidden. What may seem to be a small order that is taking three months to execute may actually be the tail end of a large order.

Accurate transaction cost measurement begins with defining an order. Many managers think that their trade order management system can define an order, but it probably does not do it correctly. Simply because a firm is trading the same name—same side, same symbol, same day—does not mean the same order is being worked. Orders may come in from different portfolio managers, for different purposes, for different traders. Likewise, some separate trades should be combined into one order. For example, the order may start out as 500 shares of a stock one day, followed by an add-on of half a million shares the next day. When does the clock start ticking? Are the two blocks the same order? Understanding the investment process and how the portfolio manager is making these decisions can help to correctly analyze the trade within the context of defining the order.

An important task in improving trade cost analysis is separating orders from dreams. Perhaps a portfolio manager had the great idea to buy a stock at $30, but it is now trading at $70. The $30 order is a dream kept on the trade list and may not be executed in the portfolio manager's lifetime. If an order is not realistic, it should be pulled out of the trading cost analysis. Otherwise, it generates enormous opportunity costs and skews the results of the analysis. Including cancel and correction logic in the analysis is critical to achieving the most accurate results. The input data have to reflect reality.

In an ideal world, all orders would have time stamps. Users can currently get good time stamps for the end of the trade, but at a minimum, the trade order management system should also provide a time stamp that indicates when the trade hit the trading desk. And for the best trading cost measurement, the trade order management system should

Figure 1. Prudential Financial, 14–18 June 2002

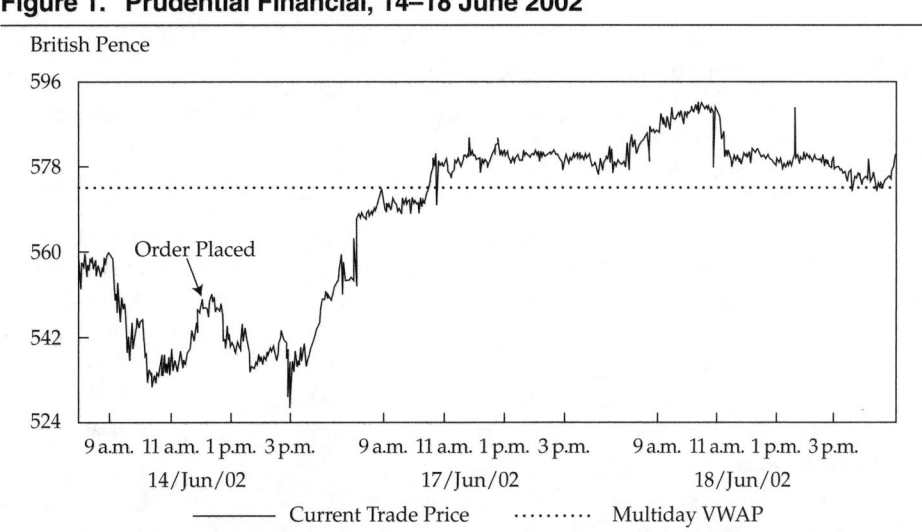

Note: Data are for trading on the LSE.

Table 1. Execution of Prudential Order, 14 June 2002 through 18 June 2002

Trade Date and Time	Side	Shares	Price (pence)
14 June 2002 16:22:00	Buy	126,742	539.4831
17 June 2002 16:44:00	Buy	165,780	575.8040
17 June 2002 16:49:00	Buy	165,779	574.8600
18 June 2002 16:40:00	Buy	573,508	578.8371

also show when the trade was initiated by the portfolio manager. Ideally, it will also tell when the trade arrived at the broker's desk. Those precise time stamps greatly improve cost measurement because, for example, time stamps can be used to separate the source of costs among desk delay, timing decisions, and market impact.

Realistically, perfect trade cost measurement is not possible; what really matters is the process. A stringent process is akin to physical exercise. Regular trips to the gym may not create an Olympic athlete but will improve overall physical performance.

Analysis

Two trading execution case studies provide analysis of and insight into the differences between the implementation shortfall and VWAP methods for measuring trading costs.

In the first case, the trader had a bad quarter. **Table 2** shows a weighted-average cost of 289.749 bps, which is considerable because 150 bps was one standard deviation away from the mean during that period.

The details, however, indicate what happened. No matter how long or short the trading list, a few trades can make all the difference in the cost analysis. For a proper analysis, it is important to consider the pattern of the trades that are incurring high costs. Is it a few trades or a lot of trades? Does a consistent pattern emerge? **Table 3** shows that three trades (Lowe's Companies, Applied Materials, and Bank of New York Company) constituted the bulk of the trading costs on the trading list, although the three trades were not large in terms of the number of

Table 2. Average Trading Cost for All Trades

Measure	Weighted-Average Cost per Share	Weighted-Average ITG ACE Cost per Share	Weighted-Average Net Cost (bps)	Profit/Loss
All	−0.518	0.018	−289.749	−$534,710,800
Market				
NYSE	−0.838	0.02	−332.001	−436,545,800
Nasdaq	−0.199	0.016	−185.031	−98,165,000
Side				
Buy	−0.71	0.02	−371.686	−471,865,500
Sell	−0.178	0.015	−109.125	−62,845,300

Note: Last/Open (T + 0 h + 0:00) Order/Primary/ACE.

Table 3. Average Trading Cost by Individual Stock

Company	Weighted-Average Cost per Share	Weighted-Average ITG ACE Cost per Share	Weighted-Average Net Cost per Share	Weighted-Average Net Cost (bps)	Profit/Loss
Lowe's Cos.	−4.19	0.017	−4.173	−118815	−$395,162,400
Applied Materials	−0.508	0.012	−0.496	−40286.5	−119,764,100
Bank of New York Co.	−0.692	0.023	−0.67	−29131.2	−75,488,700
Tyco International	−0.1	0.01	−0.09	−5823.5	−5,732,200
Merrill Lynch & Co.	−0.05	0.019	−0.031	−936.8	−3,133,600
Internet Security Systems	−0.099	0.042	−0.058	−4312.4	−2,009,200
Southwest Airlines Co.	−0.03	0.024	−0.006	−520.3	−518,200
State Street Corp.	−0.04	0.015	−0.025	−680.6	−15,000

Note: Last/Open (T + 0 h + 0:00) Order/Primary/ACE.

shares. In this case, the trades were expensive because they were part of a liquidation, where the trader sold the shares as quickly as possible without regard for market impact. When those three trades are pulled out of the trading cost analysis, the trader's performance is actually good.

Some trading costs are beyond the control of the trading desk. Those costs should not skew the results of the analysis. The cost analysis should provide good feedback on where in the investment-decision process the costs are occurring. The trading desk can then target those areas for its cost improvement efforts.

In the second case, the trader is beating all of the benchmarks, albeit modestly, in a deteriorating market. How is she doing it? Is it the result of a couple of trades? Does some pattern in the trades exist?

By comparing the trades on a days-to-completion basis, as shown in **Figure 2**, a pattern is obvious. The trader delayed execution on the buy orders as the market fell and completed execution on the sell orders quickly. Although this was a successful strategy under the circumstances, the market can reverse direction, and the trader must be able to move swiftly to adjust her strategy. Figure 2 is measured using the implementation shortfall method. If VWAP methodology is used instead, as shown in **Figure 3**, information about the trader's strategy of spreading out the buy orders in a falling market environment is hidden. VWAP smoothes out the trends in the trader's execution of orders and hides the trader's execution strategy.

Control

Accurate trading cost analysis provides the mechanism to understand and thus control trading costs. Take the case of a manager of a trading desk who regularly reviews trade cost analysis. The analysis divides the trades into meaningful categories—market, sector, days to completion, average daily volume—which allows him to look for patterns in the executions. In this case, average trading costs are high, 135 bps, on an implementation shortfall basis. **Figure 4** shows the percentage of average daily volume traded in a security. The good news is that on the difficult trades where the order represents between 100 percent and 1,000 percent of average daily volume, the traders are doing a great job. Such big, illiquid trades, however, are rare. Instead, the small trades, where the order represents between 1 percent and 5 percent of average daily volume, are much more common. The traders are getting hurt on these little trades. Although the losses on each one are small, the overall cost for trading is high and the traders' performance is mediocre.

In this particular case, when the portfolio manager wanted to raise cash, the manager chose to do a program trade, selling a slice of the portfolio (i.e., selling a small percentage of each position) in lieu of changing the portfolio composition, thus resulting in many small sell orders being sent for immediate execution. The traders need to focus on improving their performance on these types of orders. Passive trading strategies, such as limits, pegging, and strategy servers, and fewer nondiscretionary trades can help eliminate costly executions and lower total trading costs.

Figure 2. Performance by Side and Days to Completion

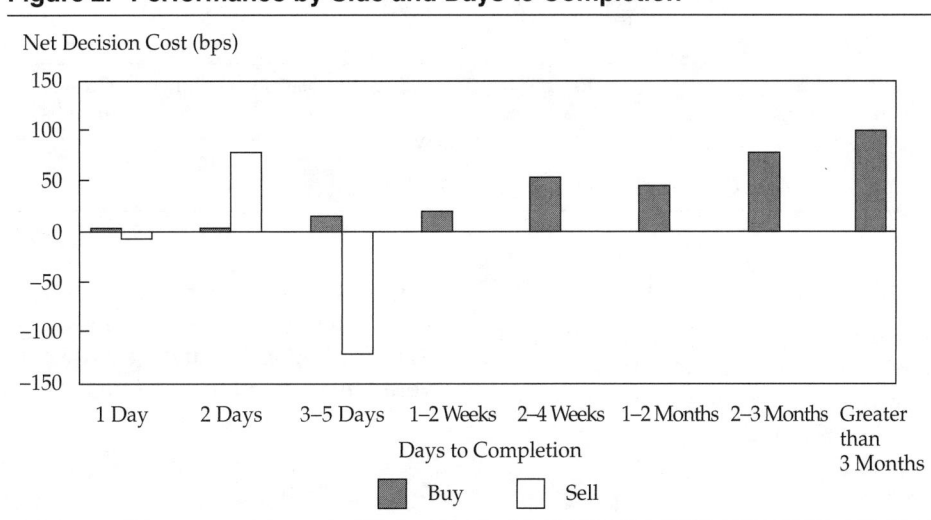

Figure 3. Buy and Sell Performance vs. VWAP

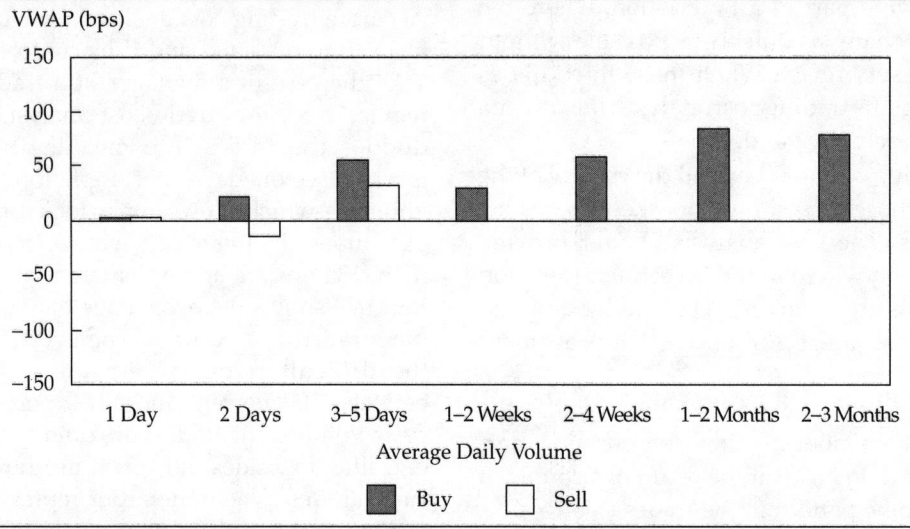

Figure 4. Actual Less Predicted Costs by Average Daily Volume

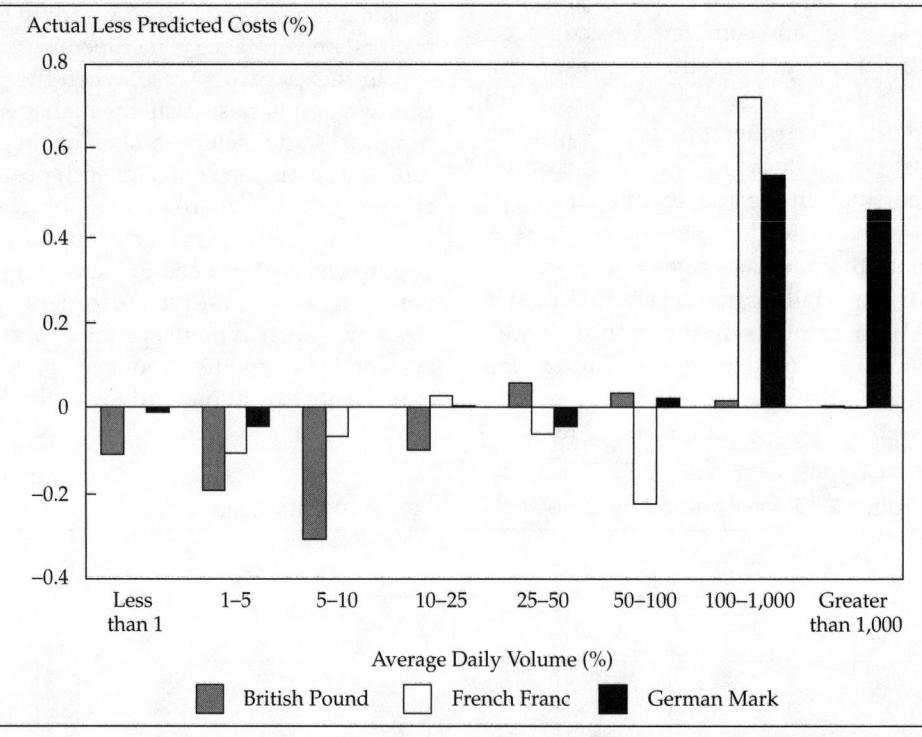

Conclusion

Transaction costs matter, and they can be controlled through measurement and analysis. The key is to measure and analyze trading costs regularly, while the memory is still fresh, and then to compare the results against a meaningful benchmark. Careful analysis will show patterns and reveal controllable costs. Finding and reducing those costs can enhance overall investment management performance.

Institutional Order Flow and the Hurdles to Superior Performance

Wayne H. Wagner
Co-Founder and Chairman
Plexus Group, Inc.
Los Angeles

> Institutional investors trade in the same markets as retail investors, but typically, institutional investors work with much larger amounts of dollars and shares. These large trades do not appear to be cost-effective when evaluated from various perspectives, which raises the question: Is trading cost related to liquidity demand or to market frictions?

Trading can be analyzed on a micro level, which is what transpires on a trading desk on a day-to-day basis. My presentation, however, will consider trading from a macro level—what the markets are like, the overall viewpoint of institutional trading, how market structure affects trading, and how well managers can control costs.

Example of a Large Institutional Trade

To a retail investor, the market may seem like a vending machine: One walks up, puts in coins, pushes a button, and walks away with the selected stock. But that is certainly not what the market looks like to the institutional trader.

Consider this real-life institutional trade. On 21 November 2002 at 8:50 a.m., a portfolio manager for a large momentum manager sent his trader an order to buy 1,745,640 shares of Oracle Corporation stock. The desk fed that order to the trade management interface, Bloomberg B-Trade, one of the several electronic communications networks (ECNs) available to the trade desk. The trading began at 9:53 a.m., slightly longer than an hour after the order was received. The order was completed in 51 minutes with 1,014 separate executions; the average execution size was about 1,700 shares. That 1,700 number is significant, as will be shown later. The largest single execution was 63,871 shares in a cluster of a total of 190,000 shares

that traded within one minute. The smallest execution was 13 shares. In this order, 17 percent of the executions were for 100 shares or less; 44 percent were for less than 1,000 shares. This order went through with up to 153 executions per minute, faster than any human could handle.

On that day, Oracle traded 59 million shares, and this 1,700,000 order represented less than 3 percent of Oracle's trading volume that day. Oracle opened on 21 November at $10.86 per share. The average price of execution was $11.01. After this order was completed, the price rose to close at $11.46. The cost of delay plus market impact, the difference between Oracle's price at the time the order was received and the average execution price, was 14 cents a share. A per share commission of a penny was charged in addition to the delay and impact cost.

Overall, this appears to be a fine trade. The loss of profit between when the portfolio manager wanted to do the trade and the time it was completed was 15 cents. The performance gained from the average price of execution to the close that day was roughly 45 cents. Thus, the ratio of the benefit of the order to the cost of completing it was three to one.

The Meat-Grinder Effect

The Oracle trade shows that it is possible to complete large illiquid trades both in the central market and in the peripheral ECN-like markets. But even in this case, a 1,000:1 reduction from order size to trade size—from 1,700,000 shares to 1,700—was needed to execute the order. This number, 1,700 shares, just

---

Editor's note: This presentation was given at the preconference workshop.

happens to be the average execution size on the NYSE. It also happens to be roughly the average trade size on Nasdaq. This average execution size is tiny compared with the size of the orders that most institutional traders handle on a daily basis.

The result is what I call the "meat-grinder" effect: Large trades have to be disaggregated into a series of smaller trades for execution. If the small trade size is the minimum matched size between the average buyer and the average seller, then institutional traders are dealing in a retail-structured market in which the institutions tiptoe around the periphery looking for trading opportunities. Alternatively, the smaller trade size could result from structural elements in the operation of the marketplace that force trades to be broken down for execution.

Think of the situation this way: To get a 1,700,000-share trade done, it must be forced through a constriction averaging 1,700 shares wide. This process stretches out the time needed to execute the trade. Meanwhile, information is leaking slowly into the marketplace, drawing the prying eyes of dealers and other market insiders. The resulting delay in executing the order translates into a search cost that raises the effective transaction cost of the trade. Such a marketplace is neither an efficient nor an effective way to transact. This inefficiency results in higher capital costs to the companies issuing stock and lower investment performance to investors. Who benefits?—market insiders who are positioned to take advantage of the fact that buyers in size have difficulty meeting directly and anonymously with sellers in size.

In order to put transaction costs into proper context, managers need to know the true costs of implementing their investment ideas. If a manager correctly anticipates that her idea will result in a doubling of value, the appreciation will more than offset the transaction costs. But if her average return per stock is only 3 percent, then transaction costs can overwhelm the benefits of the idea. Suddenly, the meat-grinder effect takes on extreme importance with today's lowered market return expectations and the challenge presented to outperform.

Frictional costs can negatively affect investors' ability to accumulate financial assets. Therefore, marketplaces need to assess their ability to provide facilities that are *efficient* (i.e., low cost from an operational standpoint), *deep* (i.e., low impact associated with the accumulation of larger positions), *liquid* (i.e., low delay costs), and *fair* (i.e., the value of research flows to those who do the research rather than to those who are able to interposition themselves in the marketplace). Today's markets do well on the first criterion but not as well on the others.

Finally, as the AIMR Trade Management Guidelines say, the costs of trading cannot be evaluated outside the context of the value of trading activity because costs are incurred in exchange for anticipated outperformance.[1]

The Plexus Study

At the end of 2002, we at the Plexus Group completed a study of transaction costs.[2] The study included 867,321 orders from the fourth quarter of 2001 and the first quarter of 2002, an up market. As a follow-up, we added 431,539 orders from the down-market second quarter of 2002. The data came from the trade accounting systems of 93 money managers linked to order records in their order management systems. Thus, we knew when the portfolio manager released the trade and when and at what average price the trade was executed. Therefore, we could measure trading costs with a fair degree of accuracy.

Institutional traders are aware that the distribution of trade size is highly skewed. A large number of small orders is mixed in with far fewer, but more significant, large orders. To account for this skew in our analysis, we sorted our entire database by dollars executed from the smallest trade to the largest. We then broke the dataset into five parts so that *each part represented the same number of dollars traded*. Because each of these five parts represents the same number of dollars traded, investors should be equally interested in the costs and performance of each of these groups. These groups, however, are quite different from one another.

At Plexus, we think of transaction costs as an iceberg, as illustrated in **Figure 1**. The commission (5 cents, or 17 bps) and impact (10 cents, or 34 bps) costs, the parts of the iceberg above the waterline, are obvious to investors. What might not be obvious are the parts of the iceberg below the waterline: the costs of delay (23 cents, or 77 bps) and missed trades (9 cents, or 29 bps). Note that the delay costs are by far the largest cost. Delay is the cost associated with having to push a large order through that 1,700-share order constriction, stretching the trade out over time in order to be able to execute it. All the while, information is leaking into the market.

In our study, we wanted to pinpoint the cost of interacting with the market. Thus, we did not include the cost of missed trades or commissions. We defined the cost of interacting in the market as the average

---
[1] The AIMR Trade Management Guidelines can be accessed at www.aimr.org/pdf/standards/trademgmt_guidelines.pdf.
[2] I would like to thank Meei-Tsern Jeng and Ali Jahansouz for their contributions to this study.

Figure 1. Iceberg of Transaction Costs

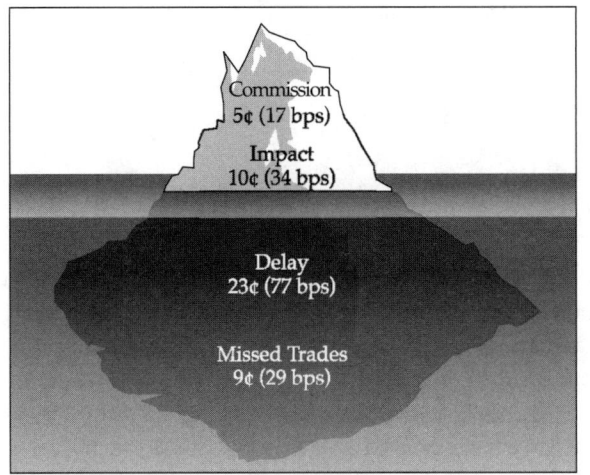

Note: Missed trade costs average 130 bps on 8 percent of the portfolio and are expressed in terms of portfolio effect.

Source: Based on data from Plexus Group.

cost of executed trades less the average decision cost. Simply stated:

Trade cost = Execution price – Decision price.

If multiple orders in the same stock came from portfolio managers, we aggregated the orders and the executions to determine the two equation variables, execution price and decision price.

Impact of Trade Size. The majority of our analyses focused on the first subperiod—the rising market. The importance of trade size in falling markets will be covered later in this presentation.

Table 1 shows some of our data for this first subperiod, the fourth quarter 2001 through the first quarter 2002. Note that 11 out of every 12 trades, or 92.5 percent of the shares traded, fell in the first quintile. The average trade size in this quintile was 2,000 shares, the average dollar amount traded was approximately $50,000, and the average trade was much less than a day's volume (0.4 percent). Furthermore, the average trade cost little to execute (11 bps). These easy-to-complete trades represent the bulk of institutional trading in terms of number of orders being processed.

In contrast, 80 percent of the dollars being traded were in the second through fifth quintiles, yet these trades represented only 7.5 percent of the orders and executions. The fifth quintile, the 20 percent of the dollars being traded as part of the largest trades, contained only 2,500 buys and sells. The average trade size was more than 2 million shares, and the average trade involved more than $75 million in principal. These trades constituted more than half a day's volume, and the costs were significantly higher than for the small trades in the first quintile. The larger trades represented only 1 out of every 400 trades, although the cost per dollar traded rose from 11 bps for the smallest trades to 90 bps for the largest trades.

That cost differential is determined by the trade size in conjunction with the market environment in which the traders have to operate. The following question then arises: Is this differential a liquidity cost proportional to the trade size, or is it a frictional cost proportional to the length of time that these trades have to be worked into the marketplace?

Notice that selling is always cheaper than buying except for in the fifth quintile. These large sell trades typically represent situations where bad news is in the market and the manager is anxious to dump the stock.

Table 2 sorts the same data another way. Each quintile was divided into percentiles of cost distribution. Remember that the 95th percentile contains those adverse momentum trades in which the trader is buying a stock that is moving up aggressively, so finding liquidity is difficult. By contrast, the fifth percentile includes those trades made under favorable market conditions, as when a trader is buying a stock that is falling in price. The table shows that the cost of execution not only increases as more

Table 1. Equal Dollar Quintiles in Rising Market: Fourth Quarter 2001 through First Quarter 2002

Trade-Size Quintile	Trade Count Buy	Trade Count Sell	Shares (000—median) Buy	Shares (000—median) Sell	Dollars (millions—median) Buy	Dollars (millions—median) Sell	Percent Average Daily Volume (median) Buy	Percent Average Daily Volume (median) Sell	Cost (bps—median) Buy	Cost (bps—median) Sell
1 (small)	444,485	356,053	2	2	0.05	0.06	0.4	0.3	–11	–6
2	22,906	18,988	154	176	4.82	5.79	10.8	11.1	–47	–36
3	8,340	7,217	393	430	13.74	15.61	18.3	18.2	–64	–47
4	3,527	3,199	851	923	31.86	35.24	28.1	30.8	–81	–69
5 (large)	1,303	1,209	2,014	2,105	75.62	80.91	52.6	53.8	–90	–127

Table 2. Cost Range of Institutional Buying in Rising Market

Trade-Size Quintile	Trade Count	Percentiles of Cost Distribution				
		5th	25th	50th	75th	95th
1 (small)	444,485	–369 bps	–82 bps	–11 bps	29 bps	240 bps
2	22,906	–689	–185	–47	29	376
3	8,340	–732	–218	–64	29	443
4	3,527	–842	–266	–81	41	588
5 (large)	1,303	–979	–328	–90	107	934

dollars are traded; the range of costs widens as trades get larger.

Impact of Other Factors. Trade size is important not only in its own right but also because of how it interacts with other factors, including the market environment in which the trade is executed, the stock's price performance, and the time needed to complete the execution of the order.

■ *Exchanges.* To understand the effect of trade size on execution cost relative to the different exchanges, we began by comparing our database with data from the NYSE *2002 Fact Book*.[3] As shown in **Table 3**, 85 percent of the orders on the NYSE are less than 2,100 shares per trade, whereas in our database of money managers, 46 percent of the trades were for 2,100 shares or less. Table 3 also shows that for the institutional sample, the percentage of dollars traded for trades of 5,000 shares or less is much lower than the figures in the NYSE data. In our data, the larger the trade size, the greater the aggregate total of dollars that were being traded. In the NYSE data, however, the percentage of dollars traded does not scale up with order size. Thus, it would seem that the exchange is largely set up for retail trading. The fact that institutions have to trade there seems almost an afterthought. Note the bulge of 45 percent of the dollars traded on the NYSE falls in the order size between 5,000 and 10,000 shares. Those trades carry the earmarks of institutional investors breaking their orders into digestible pieces.

Table 4 shows a comparison of institutional trading on the NYSE and the Nasdaq. The "Percent Excess Cost" column shows the Nasdaq cost expressed as a percentage of the NYSE cost. In the first quintile, buying in a rising market was 69 percent more expensive on the Nasdaq than on the NYSE and selling was three times as high on the Nasdaq as on the NYSE. Notice that the cost ratio falls steadily as the size of the order increases, for both buys and sells, in both rising and falling markets. The inference is that small trades are at a disadvantage on the Nasdaq as compared with the NYSE during this time period. For the fifth-quintile large trades, execution costs in the two markets were fairly comparable in a rising market. But in a falling market, the fifth-quintile buy trades illustrate an ability to buy the plunging Nasdaq stocks very cheaply.

■ *Stock-price performance.* The purpose of trading is to implement the decision to buy or sell a particular stock. **Table 5** shows the results of stock picking by portfolio managers and security analysts, not activity by traders. The column labeled "6 Weeks Post-Trade" shows the price change in the 30 trading days after the trade was made. All quintiles show stronger

---
[3] The NYSE *2002 Fact Book* can be accessed at www.nysedata.com/factbook/main.asp.

Table 3. Distribution of Trades by Order Size: Plexus Institutional Manager Database Compared with NYSE

	Order Size						
Data Source	Less than 2,100	2,500 to 5,000	5,000 to 10,000	10,000 to 25,000	25,000 to 100,000	100,000 to 250,000	More than 250,000
Percentage of orders							
Managers	46.2%	13.7%	9.5%	10.3%	11.2%	5.6%	4.1%
NYSE	84.9	7.6	3.9	2.6	0.9	0.8	0.02
Percentage of dollars traded							
Managers	1.1%	1.2%	17.6%	4.4%	18.6%	21.6%	35.4%
NYSE	12.9	4.2	44.5	6.9	9.2	21.3	1.1

Source: Based on data from Plexus Institutional Manager Database and NYSE *2002 Fact Book*.

Table 4. NYSE vs. Nasdaq Quintiles: Median Cost of Trading

Trade-Size Quintile	Buy NYSE	Buy Nasdaq	Percent Excess Cost	Sell NYSE	Sell Nasdaq	Percent Excess Cost
Rising market						
1 (small)	–8 bps	–21 bps	169%	–3 bps	–15 bps	400%
2	–38	–77	101	–27	–70	159
3	–58	–88	52	–38	–99	161
4	–78	–96	23	–62	–105	69
5 (large)	–90	–87	–3	–121	–175	45
Falling market						
1 (small)	–4	–10	150	–6	–21	250
2	–19	–34	79	–35	–88	151
3	–28	–38	36	–49	–115	135
4	–29	–12	–59	–101	–192	90
5 (large)	–19	58	–405	–143	–238	66

Table 5. Median Buying Minus Selling Price Changes for Various Time Periods

Trade-Size Quintile	5 Days Pretrade Buys	5 Days Pretrade Sells	1 Day Pretrade Buys	1 Day Pretrade Sells	5 Days Post-Trade Buys	5 Days Post-Trade Sells	6 Weeks Post-Trade Buys	6 Weeks Post-Trade Sells
1 (small)	0.50 pps	0.65 pps	0.09 pps	0.16 pps	0.86 pps	0.57 pps	3.73 pps	3.20 pps
2	0.58	0.24	0.24	–0.13	1.22	–0.16	3.26	2.01
3	0.39	0.03	0.29	–0.19	1.38	–0.18	3.34	1.86
4	0.46	–0.24	0.32	–0.44	1.47	–0.32	2.91	1.59
5 (large)	0.42	–0.79	0.27	–0.34	1.16	–1.05	2.32	0.00

performance of the buys than of the sells. But from the first to fifth quintile, the difference between the performance of the buys and the sells exhibits greater disparity. At the end of six weeks, the median fifth-quintile buying decision experienced a price change of 2.32 percentage points (pps) versus no price change for the median selling decision in the same group.

Table 5 shows that a change in the price of a stock typically occurs within six weeks of the trade, whether a buy or a sell. This time frame is much shorter than the horizon typically used by portfolio managers as they make buy/sell decisions. Note also the pretrade columns, which indicate that managers buy stocks whose price is already rising and sell ones whose price is already falling. Thus, traders encounter adverse conditions much more frequently than they encounter favorable conditions.

The good news is that buys always outperform sells except on the smallest trades in the shortest time frames. The buy/sell differential increases with the size of the trade. For a large trade, it establishes in a week and sustains for at least six months.

Similar to Table 2, **Table 6** shows a distribution, but it is a distribution of returns rather than of costs. The larger the trade, the worse the performance of the stock—a rather strange phenomenon. Our assumption had been that the big trades would be the ones for which the managers were firmly convinced of their investment ideas and thus willing to place large positions into their portfolios. The data do not support that assumption. Rather, information that causes price

Table 6. Range of 30-Day Returns for Institutional Buys

Trade-Size Quintile	Trade Count	5th	25th	50th	75th	95th
1 (small)	444,485	–22.9 pps	–4.3 pps	3.7 pps	11.8 pps	31.0 pps
2	22,906	–24.0	–5.0	3.3	11.8	30.5
3	8,340	–23.1	–4.6	3.3	11.0	28.0
4	3,527	–23.2	–4.9	2.9	10.0	25.3
5 (large)	1,303	–24.2	–5.2	2.3	10.1	25.2

movement is a strong motivator for managers to spring into action. If a portfolio manager is asked why an idea is actionable today when it was not yesterday, the typical response is that she had been thinking about the stock for a long time and waiting for a signal to indicate whether her idea was right or wrong. Good or bad news becomes a triggering motivational tool to get a trade started.

The subsequent dollar gain of a successful buying decision, plus the avoidance of the subsequent dollar loss of a successful selling decision, is the costless value that a shareholder in a fully invested fund receives as a result of a manager's decisions. Because trading is costly, implementing the decisions will produce a negative effect on the portfolio unless a performance differential exists between the buy and the sell that is larger than the cost of implementing the decision. Table 2 shows that managers pay a lot more to execute large trades than small trades, and Table 6 shows that even before transaction costs, large trades are not justified in terms of expected return. The frequently used adage "paying away the alpha" comes to mind.

To determine if these large trades are motivated by information or a need for liquidity, we divided the five quintiles according to whether they were less than 25 percent, 50 to 100 percent, or more than 100 percent of the daily volume. Within each quintile, the median dollars traded did not vary much across the groupings by daily volume (i.e., the trade size was roughly the same irrespective of how large the trades were as a percentage of daily volume). Thus, managers do not seem to be paying attention to marketplace liquidity as they make their trading decisions. Given the cost structure documented previously, that practice does not seem totally rational.

The following analysis is mathematically incorrect—adding and subtracting medians is not strictly correct, although the errors induced should be small—but it may be insightful. **Table 7** shows the round-trip return benefit from trading. It was computed as follows: First, we computed the costless marginal return of the activity by adding together the (median) buying decision return in each category and the (median) selling decision return. Then, we subtracted the combined (median) buying cost and the combined (median) selling cost. The resulting number is the change in performance experienced by investors after accounting for the trading cost. The numbers in bold show the time frame in which that differential is maximized. Although Table 7 follows the trade out to 125 days, most of the value-added price action occurs over a fairly short-term horizon.

Several conclusions can be stated. First, the information that managers and security analysts use to make buy/sell decisions embeds itself in the stock price fairly rapidly. Second, the cost of execution is important in a trading environment that favors small trades and thus disadvantages institutional investors. If delay costs, which average 71 bps, can be avoided, the impact on portfolio performance is substantial and favorable. Thus, we must conclude that the current structure of the market largely consumes the value of the investment decision through implementation costs and is not well suited to the needs of institutional trading.

■ *Time to execute.* Peeking into the fifth quintile of the largest trades, we observed that these orders, which average about half a day's trading volume, took longer than a day to complete for 94 percent of the buys and 93 percent of the sells. Interestingly, the average percentage complete was about 92 percent for buys and about 93 percent for sells, which implies that about 8 percent of the orders were left on the desk unexecuted because the price had moved to the point where the manager became uninterested in completing the trade.

Table 8 looks closely at the trades that cannot be completed in one day. For the largest trades (fifth quintile), only 7 percent were completed in one day or less; 93 percent required more than one day to complete. Surely, a qualified trader would complete these trades quickly if it were possible. The extended time horizon needed to complete these trades results from the fact that liquidity is not readily available. To draw out liquidity, the trader has to signal trading interest to the market. Once that information becomes known, however, the market frequently starts running in front of the trader. The price starts moving, and the trader cannot get the trade done. The result is delay, also known as search, costs.

Down-Market Results. The second period in our sample was a down market, the second quarter of 2002. **Figure 2** contrasts the buying and selling costs in both up and down markets for each volume quintile. Table 1 showed that in rising markets selling is cheaper than buying except for the largest trades. In a down market, however, the phenomenon is

Table 7. Median Percentage Return Differential Less Median Round-Trip Costs

Trade-Size Quintile	1 Day	5 Days	30 Days	125 Days
1 (small)	0.03 pps	0.12 pps	**0.36 pps**	0.25 pps
2	0.23	**0.54**	0.42	–0.53
3	–0.02	**0.45**	0.37	–0.64
4	–0.25	**0.28**	–0.19	–0.92
5 (large)	–0.75	0.04	**0.15**	–0.62

Note: Numbers in bold show where the differential maximizes.

Table 8. Trading Duration by Order Size

Trade-Size Quintile/ Trading Duration	Number of Orders	Done in One Day	Cap ($ billions)	Percent Volume	Cost (bps)	Order Size (000 shares)
1 (small)						
One day	342,300	77%	3	0.3	−8	1
More than one day	102,185	23	3	1.4	−40	8
2						
One day	8,331	36	10	7	−28	133
More than one day	14,575	64	5	16	−74	170
3						
One day	2,036	24	18	11	−39	342
More than one day	6,304	76	9	23	−83	408
4						
One day	510	14	32	16	−48	681
More than one day	3,017	86	15	32	−96	881
5 (large)						
One day	85	7	26	27	−15	1,974
More than one day	1,218	93	27	54	−99	2,030

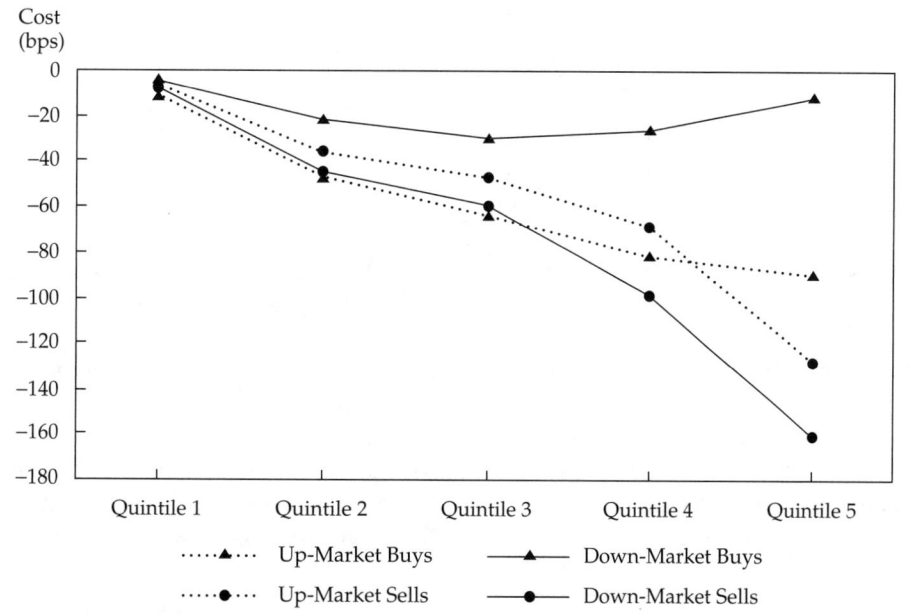

Figure 2. Up- and Down-Market Comparisons

reversed: The cost of buying in down markets drops for the fifth-quintile trades, almost reaching the cost level of the small trades in the first quintile. The lesson is that those who are willing to supply liquidity by buying in a falling market benefit by receiving low transaction costs.

Clearly, market direction defines whether trades are liquidity consuming, which infers they will be costly because liquidity must be bought on the market, or liquidity providing, which leads to inexpensive trading because the liquidity demander pays up for the liquidity. Note that these conditions are different and do not seem to counterbalance each other in the marketplace. The gains to liquidity providers fall short of the losses incurred by liquidity demanders, and these frictional costs seem to grow at a faster rate than trade size grows.

Herding

A major subject of interest in the market is whether institutional investors exhibit herding behavior. That is, do institutional investors buy the same stock at the same time and sell the same stock at the same time?

To investigate the question of herding, we analyzed the activity of the managers in the database who traded in Tyco International stock. We picked Tyco because the stock was in an extended swan dive from January through June 2002. The greatest selling activity in the database corresponded with and followed slightly the largest stock-price drops. Managers thus appeared to react to information—information that could not be forecasted. Among the news events was the following: On 29 January 2002, Tyco announced that it paid a director for arranging the acquisition of the CIT finance unit, and immediately afterward, roughly 32 million shares were sold by the managers in the database. On 25 April 2002, Tyco announced that it was dropping its break-up plan and was cutting 7,100 jobs, and again, immediately afterward, about 27 million shares were sold.

We looked at the three days surrounding Tyco's announcement on 25 April 2002. We divided the sample into diversified managers, momentum managers, and value managers, as shown in **Table 9**. We found that 31 of the managers were buying and 51 were selling. Only 8 million shares were bought, whereas 55 million shares were sold. Using an implementation shortfall approach, we found that those who bought did well. Those who sold, however, did not do as well, particularly in terms of transaction costs. Curiously, the momentum managers had the lowest trading costs, probably because they follow a more aggressive trading strategy. They traded faster and thus experienced less delay costs. In the three-day period surrounding the 25 April announcement, three managers bought more than once, six managers sold more than once, and nine managers both bought and sold in these three days. Thus, herding does not appear to be taking place. In fact, other than the preponderance of reactive selling on bad news, managing behavior is more like herding cats!

Conclusion

Many markets are characterized by a volume discount. Buying 100,000 pounds of milk, for example, is less costly per gallon than buying an eight-pound, one-gallon jug. The volume discount primarily reflects the combination of market power and economies of scale in delivery. In terms of clearing the trade, it is hard to see why a thousand- or hundred-thousand-share trade for an institutional investor would be significantly more costly to process than a one-share trade. Yet, economies of scale do not seem to apply in the market for equity securities: The evidence suggests that large trades cost more, even though the level of intermediary hazard is small.

Rather than focus on economies of scale, examination of the incentives of the participants in the market is needed. No one wants to execute early against a large, informed trader. But the market makers' motivation is not to avoid trading with parties who combine valuable research insights with trading size. Rather, their motivation seems oriented toward creating profit opportunities by keeping large buyers and sellers from interacting directly and anonymously.

Assuredly, some cost is inevitable and an unavoidable consequence of liquidity demand in massive size. Yet, managers pay up for size even though the information value is not there. This practice is evidence of "lucrative friction"—unnecessary interpositioning and leakage to prying eyes, resulting in delay, which is costly.

Our analysis supports the hypothesis that trading costs are more related to endogenous market frictions, in which costs are proportional to time to execute, than they are to immediacy demand stemming from exogenous superior research.

Trading costs are real. Many are unavoidable consequences of liquidity and size. Just because someone wants to buy 2 million shares does not mean that someone else wants to sell 2 million shares.

Table 9. Tyco Trading by Manager Style for Three-Day Window around 25 April 2002

Item	Diversified	Momentum	Value	Total
Buy				
Number of managers	20	8	3	31
Shares (million)	1	6	1	8
Average cost (bps)	276	710	521	—
Sell				
Number of managers	30	15	6	51
Shares (million)	31	18	6	55
Average cost (bps)	−225	−180	−239	—

Sometimes, liquidity has to be found and coaxed out into the market. Every buy-side trader wants to see without being seen, but advertising the desire to trade is necessary for finding the liquidity in the market. Advertising, however, causes an information leakage. Much anecdotal evidence of this lucrative friction exists.

Instinet, Liquidnet, Harborside, POSIT, and Jefferies are among many extensively used crossing systems. They are useful solutions to the problem of filling institutional-size orders, but they are only a partial answer. More work needs to be done. Trustworthy human intelligence is needed at the core of the market. The solutions will come forth only in response to demand from money owners and investors.

As John Phelan, former chairman of the NYSE, said in 1989, "Technology and communication bring efficiency. Money is made in inefficiency." I hope he was joking. Our evidence suggests that those who raise capital in the markets pay too much for it, whereas those who invest in the markets earn too little from knowledgeable, professional management.

Equity Trading: Execution and Analysis

Question and Answer Session

Jennifer Conrad
Marie S. Konstance, CFA
Wayne H. Wagner

Question: Do firms rely on one trader's benchmark exclusively, or do they use multiple measures of performance?

Konstance: A benchmark steers users toward a course of action. Generally, people look at several benchmarks but use just one as a primary basis for analysis. The reason is that it is impossible to win against all of them.

Sometimes, traders use different benchmarks for different types of funds. For example, they will use implementation shortfall for most of their portfolios but turn to VWAP for a particular portfolio where the manager always places orders with enormous position size and expects the trades to be done over a few days.

Question: In the Tyco example, which showed big selling activity accompanying bad news, who was trading on the opposite side of the net sales identified in the study?

Wagner: For all of those people who were selling, somebody was buying. I do not know who it was. I am sure that there was some dealer positioning, but that was moved through quickly. The activity also may have been traders buying stock to cover short positions. It would be interesting to look at what the short interest was in those days on Tyco. It had to be high.

Question: Where do the data come from? Can you tell who had the buy order and who had the sell order?

Conrad: There is an algorithm that just about everybody uses. The firm that initiated the order can often be determined by backing out the trade price relative to a quote that was posted just prior. This comparison can determine whether the order was a buy or a sell.

This process is called the Lee–Ready algorithm (named for Charles M.C. Lee and Mark Ready).[1] They matched their model with a database that contained information on who initiated the order. The results are accurate as long as the time period between when the trade was executed and when the quote occurred is limited to a range of 5–20 seconds.

Question: Has there been an increase in the number of people interested in trade analysis?

Konstance: I do see a lot of people looking at trading costs. The motivation is coming from many different directions. The U.S. SEC is one motivator, as are a firm's marketing department and compliance department because they are both interested in reducing the cost of trading.

Question: Is VWAP dead yet?

Konstance: No, I do not think so. I would say 60–70 percent of my clients are interested in implementation shortfall, but the rest of the world uses VWAP. Some good reasons exist for using it. For example, VWAP could be a reasonable measure to use in the absence of time stamps.

Wagner: I agree. The implementation shortfall approach is hard work. It takes a lot of time to calculate and requires a real understanding of the process, which has value

[1] Charles M.C. Lee and Mark Ready, "Inferring Trade Direction from Intraday Data," *Journal of Finance* (June 1991):733–746.

in and of itself. Linking up information in the order management system with the accounting records is neither obvious nor easy. There isn't a one-to-one correspondence.

VWAP is a decent measure for the 92 percent of orders that average 2,000 shares in size. There aren't many additional factors to consider in these cases. As a benchmark, VWAP gets less relevant and more questionable as the trade size gets larger. Take the extreme example of a single trading desk buying every share that traded in a given stock on a single day. That desk would be the VWAP and would appear to have excellent execution no matter what price was paid. So, there is a limit to the usefulness of VWAP.

To some extent, VWAP remains popular in the plan sponsor community, which accounts for its continued use. It is also easier to understand than implementation shortfall.

Question: Do trading desks have a disincentive to measure and publicize costs?

Wagner: No one wants to be evaluated if he or she doesn't have to be. Years ago, portfolio managers didn't have their performance measured, but today, they live and die by the sword of their performance numbers. Now, they want to know if the trading desk is doing a good job and if it can validate that performance objectively. Measuring trading costs is inevitable.

Konstance: Some traders and portfolio managers are concerned because they're afraid that the transaction cost analysis will not take into consideration the special situations that occurred in the transaction. It is important for traders to be able to show what actually happened when they traded.

But we also see an interest in transaction cost analysis as a tool to evaluate the trading process to ensure that traders are paid appropriately. Everybody cares about who is contributing to the bottom line. Trade analysis makes it possible to show that traders are adding value.

Conrad: The traders I have talked to believe that they are doing a good job. They also believe that their good work is not being recognized because their execution costs are measured with too much fuzz in them.

My concern is that the sample we used may have a selection bias in the other direction. That is, a firm has hired a consultant to look at its execution costs because it is concerned about controlling them. But those firms that don't seem to be worried about execution costs may be where the real problems exist. Because those firms are not in our data sample, we may not be getting a realistic trading population for analysis. We may be getting only the folks who already have the most controlled execution costs.

Konstance: Trading costs are going to be evaluated no matter what. Clients and management want to see trading costs, and traders want to see them too because before traders can explain these costs to anyone else, they need to understand them themselves.

Question: Has the composition of the "iceberg of trading costs" changed proportionately as the use of alternative trading systems (ATS), such as Instinet, POSIT, and Bloomberg, have increased?

Wagner: Yes, we recently redrew the iceberg chart. It now shows that the delay costs are a much larger percentage of the total and the commission costs are a bit smaller percentage. The impact costs are about the same as they have always been.

Those changes are not because of ECNs and other ATS. Instead, they are a result of two things: First, liquidity is reduced because the market is down; and second, the penny spreads and the change in the order handling rules are not beneficial to institutional investors.

The current order-handling rules make it difficult to find the pools of liquidity, a situation that has increased the delay costs. Traders have to search for liquidity with fewer mechanisms for reaching the marketplace than they had five or six years ago.

Question: Given that crossing systems and ECNs seem to perform so well, are you surprised that they aren't more popular?

Wagner: Crossing systems are a curious phenomenon. They match the smaller of the size that is offered as a buy or a sell. The hit rate seems to be somewhere around 10 percent or lower, meaning that a lot of orders are being put into crossing systems but not getting crossed.

The real problem is that there's no pricing mechanism involved. There's no way to equilibrate the supply and the demand, which is done by changing the price. If there are more buyers than sellers, the price ought to go up, right? That is the purpose of a market. Crossing systems are nice for trades that can cross, but imbalances have to go to the marketplace.

Konstance: There is confidentiality in crossing networks and systems. Note that confidentiality means not giving up any information, which is different from anonymity. There is, however, a trade-off. A crossing system has no way to set pricing.

Not all trades can be done on a crossing system, but those that are will be done at a fair rate. The rest will go to the primary market.

Conrad: Crossing systems rely on the underlying markets for price discovery and to handle volume. ECNs don't necessarily need the underlying market because they have some of those price-setting capabilities themselves.

By looking at the volume differences on Nasdaq and on ECNs, I can make a good argument that ECNs are taking trading from Nasdaq. In fact, ECNs are taking Nasdaq stocks almost exclusively while crossing systems are taking NYSE stocks, which shows the difference between how much crossing systems and ECNs rely on the underlying market to provide a clearing price. Crossing systems depend on the NYSE to provide a one-price clearing mechanism for their trades, with no need or flexibility to set price. ECNs have much more flexibility in pricing trades; in fact, a study by Roger Huang shows that ECNs play an important role in price discovery for active Nasdaq stocks.[2]

Question: What is a good (or bad) cost on an implementation shortfall and a VWAP basis? Is the real issue actual cost versus expected cost?

Konstance: When we look at the implementation shortfall, we always include expected cost. We take the actual cost and adjust it by the expected cost to get a net figure.

What is good (or bad) can vary widely. But overall, I'd say that the implementation shortfall for a large diversified fund should tend toward zero. The standard deviation has been about 150 bps either way, at least as a general rule.

Wagner: Looking for a good (or bad) number on an individual trade doesn't make a lot of sense. The data need to be aggregated to derive good information.

---
[2] Roger Huang, "The Quality of ECN and Nasdaq Market Maker Quotes," *Journal of Finance* (June 2002):1285–1319.

But there's another way to approach this issue. The AIMR TMG says that the evaluation should take place in the context of the portfolio benefit that is acquired for the cost. Any charge can be justified as long as it is not more than the value generated in performance.

If a portfolio manager's ideas are good and timely, the trading desk can spend a lot of money executing them and still do a good job for the client. But if the trading costs are high and the manager's decisions turn bad, it will be hard to justify the high costs. Costs have to be evaluated in the context of accomplishments.

Question: Trade analysis systems are highly developed in the equity sector. How do you see them developing in other asset classes, such as fixed income?

Konstance: I know trade analysis systems for fixed income are being considered, but the data are so spotty they will be difficult to evaluate. We are also getting a lot of requests for options transaction analysis systems.

Wagner: We are getting a lot of requests on the fixed-income side, and we're working to devise a basic product. Elkins/McSherry has had a product in the marketplace for awhile.

The first problem with evaluating fixed-income trading is that a string of transactions similar to that in the equity markets does not exist; the tape can't be used as a base for evaluation. The second problem is that in an equity management shop, there are clearly identified portfolio managers and clearly identified traders. The handoffs from manager to trader to broker can be timed and tracked against the market.

Fixed-income managers sit on the trading desk. A lot of ideas may be spinning in their heads, but only a small portion of those are executable. Only those trades that get done can be seen, and the related costs are hard to identify. Still, the demand is there for a fixed-income product. In the next 5–10 years, someone will determine how to make a good one.

Question: Do crossing systems just cherry pick the easy order flow?

Conrad: When we were looking at the multiple-mechanism orders, we fully expected to see that the crossing systems were used for the first trade. A trader would go in, take off that liquidity, and then move to other trading mechanisms that could satisfy the most difficult part of the order. We didn't find that in our sample.

But we studied the 1996–98 time period. At that time, prices seemed to change about every minute and a half. Crossing systems were still being used throughout a multiple-mechanism order—even until the last trade—just about as extensively as they were in the first part of the order. We didn't find much evidence of cherry picking, but the situation could be vastly different now.

Question: How are the data adjusted for such execution instructions as pure agency, agency incentive, VWAP, market on close, principal bids, and so on?

Conrad: To the extent that we had data on order instruction, we couldn't find any difference in the variables that we measured relative to those types of orders. The key problem is getting the data.

Wagner: From a procedural standpoint, we can analyze anything that we can identify. We can look at market orders and limit orders on a side-by-side basis to see the effects of trading various ways. That kind of analysis is illuminating but requires the client to identify and record the information.

Question: How can buy-side traders resist pressures to engage in soft-dollar arrangements that make the desk look bad?

Wagner: I've said many times that if the broker doesn't earn the right to the trade on a trade-by-trade basis, the execution isn't going to be as good. We have measured the effects of directed commissions, soft-dollar commissions, and wrap commissions—all of which are owed to the broker. We have found that directed commissions lead to the worst execution quality because the broker is primarily beholden to the plan sponsor and not the trader. Instead of processing the ideas through the market, the firm is required to detour trades to specific brokers.

For the 92 percent of the trades that are only 20 percent of the volume, it is hard to distinguish one broker from another. Those trades are mechanical. They are processed, as distinguished from managed. There is not, in my mind, a lot that can be added or subtracted on that level.

The wrap-fee trades are probably the hardest for a trader to manage. The wrap account may have come from a broker who doesn't have the qualifications to handle a specific trade. That leads to hard decisions for an investment management organization. I've seen organizations and trade desks try to stand up to the wrap-fee-related trading requirements, but it is tough. From the broker's perspective, much of the profit comes from securing the order flow. They are highly resistant to letting it go elsewhere.

Conrad: I co-wrote a paper in the *Journal of Finance* in 2001 using Plexus Group data.[3] Kevin Johnson, Sunil Wahal, and I looked at the difference in total costs, implementation shortfall costs, market impact, and explicit costs of

---

[3] Jennifer Conrad, Kevin M. Johnson, and Sunil Wahal, "Institutional Trading and Soft Dollars," *Journal of Finance* (February 2001):397–416.

brokers that were categorized as soft dollar, research, full service, or execution. We found that even after controlling for the special situations attached to an order and the differences in institutions sending an order, differences in execution costs existed along those four categories of brokers.

Soft-dollar brokers are about 14–16 bps per order more expensive, followed by research, full service, and execution cost brokers. Although the benefits of soft-dollar brokerage cannot be measured, there are significant costs associated with sending trades to soft-dollar brokers.

Konstance: If you can quantify your costs by the type of venue you use and the reason you trade, then you can explain it to management. You may not win that battle, but at least you have some ammunition to say "this is why it is costing me more."

Question: Have you seen an upward trend in ECN use? If so, how will buy-side institutions pay for sell-side research going forward?

Wagner: If you believe the Myners Report, purchasing sell-side research is going to become part of the cost of investment management.[4] There isn't any other industry that I know of that works the way ours does, with someone else paying for raw materials.

Firms may get the money to pay for research from higher fees or from less wasteful use of research. Most money managers do not need all the research reports that they receive anyway.

Question: What will happen if soft dollars disappear?

Wagner: In the bond market, brokers have devised ways of delivering bond research without collecting commissions for it. So, I suspect equity soft-dollar practices will similarly go underground. Attracting order flow will continue to be important to dealers, and they will determine ways to continue to do that. If that means giving recommendations on stocks and bonds, then brokers will give recommendations on stocks and bonds. Instead of soft dollars, they will get paid for it some other way.

---

[4]The Myners Report, a plan for pension industry reform, was commissioned by the U.K. government and written by Paul Myners, director of a British asset management company. The report was released in March of 2001. See also Marcus Hooper's presentation in this proceedings.

Pretrade Cost Analysis and Management of Implementation Shortfall

Minder Cheng
Global Head of Equity and Currency Trading
Barclays Global Investors
San Francisco

> Measuring trading costs entails looking at six components: commission, bid–ask spread, market trend, liquidity impact, opportunity costs, and slippage. These components combine to determine the implementation shortfall. But trade cost management requires more than just measuring completed trading costs; it requires forecasting the costs of future trades and then incorporating the forecasts into trade list generation and portfolio optimization. By measuring, forecasting, and managing trading costs, a firm can work toward the ultimate goal—best execution.

Most people say they know best execution when they see it, but my goal is to get people to focus on what can be done before the trade so that best execution can be known before it is seen. In this presentation, I will describe a process for quantifying trading performance that can be integrated into the investment decision.

One way to envision transaction cost management is as an equilateral triangle. The first side of the triangle is the measurement of post-trade performance. The second side of the triangle is forecasting, where estimates of the costs to trade are calculated. The reason to have forecasts is to incorporate the expected trading costs into the portfolio optimization process so that the costs can be managed (the third side). When the trade arrives at the trading desk, the trader's job is to manage the gap between the portfolio manager's or model's expectations of trading costs and the reality of the market in which the trader operates. The ultimate goal is to have the performance of the trading function match or beat the expectations under the model. These three sides of the triangle—measurement, forecasting, and management—form the framework of my discussion.

Measurement

An optimal trading strategy begins with the accurate measurement of trading costs and the implementation shortfall. The concept of implementation shortfall is not new. It was first raised by André Perold back in the late 1980s.[1] Over time, it has been revised, and now every investment management shop seems to have its own version.

Components of Trading Costs. Following are the quantitative components of trading costs.

■ *Commissions, fees, and taxes*. These costs are self-explanatory and unavoidable.

■ *Bid–ask spread*. If the order is small, the spread may be the only additional cost.

■ *Market trend*. When a trader is executing an order, the market may be trending in favor of or against the order. That effect needs to be factored into the trading costs, even though it is beyond the trader's and the portfolio manager's control.

■ *Liquidity impact*. Liquidity impact arises when an order is larger than the inside market or requires more immediate liquidity than liquidity providers can provide. At this point, the trade becomes visible to the rest of the market because of its size. Because of the immediate demand on liquidity, trading costs will be higher.

■ *Opportunity costs*. Opportunity costs arise when an order is not filled the same day that it hits the trading desk. Sometimes, orders take a few days to fill. Consequently, the portfolio manager is missing out on any intraday or day-by-day returns until the order is filled.

---
[1] André F. Perold, "The Implementation Shortfall: Paper vs. Reality," *Journal of Portfolio Management* (Spring 1988):4–9.

■ *Slippage.* Slippage is the difference between the price when the order is entered (benchmark price) and the closing price as of the night prior to the order being executed. In other words, it is realized opportunity costs.

Implementation Shortfall. The first step in using the implementation shortfall approach is deciding on a benchmark because the right benchmark is essential to proper portfolio performance measurement. Most people have probably heard of using volume-weighted average price (VWAP), open, close, previous close, and high–low benchmarks. For anyone running active portfolios, the proper way to benchmark is from the point when the trade list is cut. Anything that happens after the trade list is cut simply adds to or subtracts from the portfolio manager's original concept in creating the trade list. If the model is run daily, the benchmark used in most cases is the prior night's close. If the model is run intraday, the benchmark used is the point at which the trade list is regenerated.

At Barclays Global Investors, after establishing the benchmark, we look at the implementation shortfall relative to three perspectives: the paper portfolio, the actual portfolio, and the "rabbit" portfolio.

■ *Paper portfolio.* The paper portfolio is nirvana—the ideal situation. All securities are transacted at benchmark prices. Transaction costs (i.e., commissions, bid–ask spread, liquidity impact, opportunity costs, market trends, and slippage) do not happen. This model portfolio is the starting point of the analysis.

■ *Actual portfolio.* The actual portfolio reflects reality; all securities are transacted in real markets. Thus, all six of those components—market impact, commissions, bid–ask spread, liquidity, opportunity costs, and slippage—are factored in.

■ *Rabbit portfolio.* The "rabbit" portfolio represents expected trading costs; all securities are transacted in expected markets, with the six trading cost components at expected levels.[2] The paper portfolio has no trading costs. The actual portfolio has high trading costs. The rabbit portfolio's trading costs should, on average, fall somewhere between the two.

The rabbit portfolio embodies the second side of the triangle (forecasting). Whatever we learn from our actual trades is incorporated into generating our expected trading costs. So, when we cut the trade list, we have an expectation of the total cost of each of the trades on the trade list by name, by market, and by day. The rabbit portfolio is the benchmark for our traders against which their performance is measured.

■ *Summary.* The implementation shortfall is the trading cost differential between the paper portfolio and the actual portfolio. The elements of trade cost management can be conceptualized through proper decomposition and attribution of the implementation shortfall and by comparing each element with its counterpart in the rabbit portfolio.

Implementation Shortfall Measurement

The implementation shortfall can be measured several ways, as illustrated in the following examples. The order and its execution, as given in **Table 1**, are the same for all but the last example. A portfolio manager placed an order to buy 700 shares of XYZ, and the shares were bought over three days. The order was issued on Day 0 after the close. On Day 1, the trader purchased 300 shares at a price of $101.00, and the market closed that day at $102.00. On Day 2, the trader purchased an additional 200 shares at a price of $101.75; the market closed that day at $102.50. On Day 3, the day the sample period ended, the trader purchased another 100 shares at a price of $102.50, and the market closed a bit higher at $102.75. Notice that only 600 shares were executed; 100 shares were left unexecuted. For the 600 shares that were bought over three days, the average price was $101.50.

Table 1. Trading Data for Purchasing 700 Shares of XYZ

Day	Price at Close	Trade Price	Number of Shares
0	$100.00	$100.00	0
1	102.00	101.00	300
2	102.50	101.75	200
3	102.75	102.50	100

Time Analysis. The implementation shortfall for this trade over time is represented graphically in **Figure 1**. The top line is the paper portfolio return, which assumes that on Day 1, all 700 shares were traded at the previous night's (Day 0's) close of $100 a share. At the end of Day 1, when the stock closed at $102, the paper portfolio showed a $2 per share profit, for a total profit of $2 × 700, or $1,400. And because all 700 shares were traded on Day 1, on Day 2 the profit was $2.50 per share for all 700 shares ($1,750 total)—the difference between the close on Day 0 and the close on Day 2—and so on. This situation is the trading ideal.

---

[2] When designing this trade cost management process at Barclays, we kept thinking of this portfolio as experimental, like the study of a laboratory animal. Therefore, we began referring to it as the "rabbit portfolio," and the term stuck. In a sense, the actual portfolio is in a race against the rabbit portfolio.

Figure 1. Portfolio Return by Trading Day

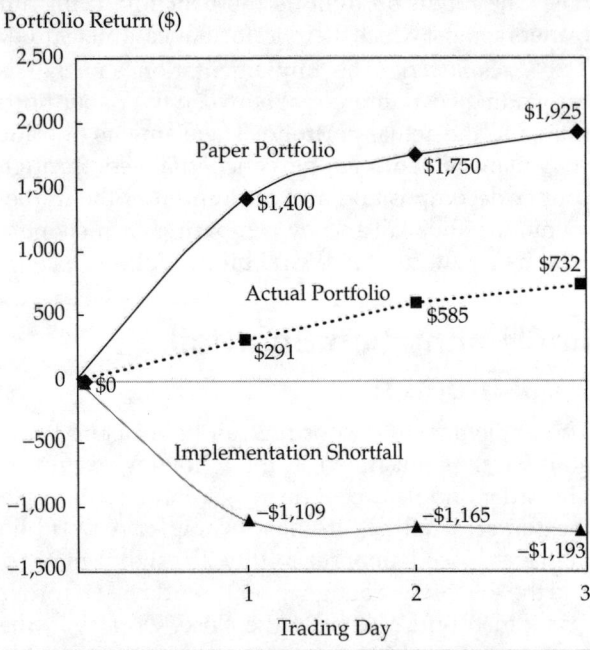

The second line graphs the actual portfolio return. On Day 1, only 300 shares were bought at $101.00, rather than at the previous day's close of $100. The $291 reflects the $1 per share profit earned on those 300 shares minus the commission of 3 cents per share. On Day 2, 200 more shares were bought at $101.75, with the profit for those shares being the Day 2 close of $102.50 less the trade price and the commission cost, for a total of $144. This amount was added to the appreciation of the 300 shares that were purchased on Day 1. Those 300 shares earned $0.50 per share (or $150) on Day 2. Therefore, the total Day 2 profit was $585—the Day 1 profit on the 300 shares ($291) plus the Day 2 profit on the 200 shares ($144) plus the incremental profit on the 300 Day 1 shares ($150). The Day 3 profit would be calculated similarly, but please keep in mind that this is a simplified example.

The implementation shortfall is the difference between the top two lines. On Day 1, the difference between the actual and paper portfolios was $1,109. On the second day, the difference was $1,165, and on the third day, it was $1,193. At its completion, therefore, the implementation shortfall on this trade was $1,193.

Profit-and-Loss Analysis. Another way to measure the implementation shortfall is in terms of profit and loss as of the Day 3 close. For the paper portfolio, the Day 3 profit was $1,925 [700 ×($102.75 – $100.00)], or 275 bps ($102.75 – $100.00). This analysis assumes that the actual portfolio paid a commission of 3 cents a share. The trade of 300 shares executed on Day 1 generated $516 in profit [300 × ($102.75 – $101.00 – $0.03)]. The trade of 200 shares executed on Day 2 generated $194 in profit [200 × ($102.75 – $101.75 – $0.03)]. And the 100 shares executed on Day 3 yielded $22 in profit [100 × ($102.75 – $102.50 – $0.03)]. So, the total profit for the trade in the actual portfolio was $732, or 105 bps. At its completion, the implementation shortfall—the difference between the paper and actual portfolios—was $1,925 – $732, which is $1,193, or 170 bps.

In contrast, the rabbit portfolio returned 100 bps.[3] In this case, the model, the rabbit portfolio, performed slightly worse in terms of profit than did the actual portfolio. Recall that the purpose of the rabbit portfolio is to have a fair comparison by which to judge the actual trade because some trades are simply difficult to execute in a given market situation. The gap between the paper and actual portfolios—a loss of close to 200 bps—shows that there was room for improvement in the actual execution of the trade, but the minimal difference in profit between the rabbit and actual portfolios is encouraging; at least the actual execution did better than our expectation.

Component Analysis. Table 2 shows yet another way to look at the implementation shortfall by analyzing each component of the implementation shortfall at the end of each trading day. Measuring the trade in this way allows for an analysis of the less

---
[3] If the model expects the 700 shares to be executed at an average price of $101.725 per share and the commission rate to be 3 cents per share, the rabbit portfolio's return would be $696.50, or 100 bps.

Table 2. Implementation Shortfall for Actual Portfolio: Example

Day	Residual	Commission	Market Impact	Slippage	Opportunity Costs
0	700	$0	$0	$0	$0
1	400	–9	–300	0	–800
2	200	–6	50	–400	–500
3	100	–3	0	–250	–275
Total	100	–$18	–$250	–$650	–$275

Note: Opportunity costs are not additive.

obvious costs of trading—market impact, slippage, and opportunity costs.

At Day 0, nothing was traded, so the residual was 700 shares. At the end of Day 1, after 300 shares were traded, the residual was 400 shares. The commission cost at the end of Day 1 was $9 (3 cents × 300 shares). The market impact (which incorporates the market trend, bid–ask spread, and liquidity impact) at the end of Day 1 was calculated as the difference between the Day 0 close ($100) and the trade price ($101.00) times the number of shares traded, or $300. The opportunity costs on Day 1 were $800—400 shares unexecuted multiplied by the price difference between the Day 0 close ($100.00) and the Day 1 close ($102.00). The opportunity costs reflect the fact that the manager was sitting on cash that was earning a zero return. Slippage did not come into play until later in the process.

On Day 2, the trader bought 200 shares more of XYZ. The residual dropped to 200 shares from 400 shares, and trading those 200 shares resulted in paying $6 more in commissions. The market impact on Day 2 was smaller than it was on Day 1 because the trade was smaller—200 shares times the Day 1 close ($102.00) minus the Day 2 trade price ($101.75), or $50. The market impact was in the trader's favor on Day 2 because the Day 2 trade price was lower than the Day 1 close. The opportunity costs equaled the residual on Day 2 (200 shares) times the difference between the Day 0 close ($100.00) and the Day 2 close ($102.50), or $500. Half of the prior day's opportunity costs (½ of $800 = $400) can be considered slippage to reflect the portion of opportunity costs that became realized through partial execution of the 400 shares.

At the end of Day 3, the residual was 100 shares, with 600 shares successfully purchased. The trading costs for the execution of the 600 shares over the three-day period included a total of $18 in commissions, $250 in market impact, $650 in slippage, and $275 in opportunity costs. The opportunity costs were not additive because each day's opportunity costs were updated based on the latest residual shares and price. At its completion, the total cost, or implementation shortfall, was $1,193. This amount is exactly the same implementation shortfall I found by comparing the difference between the paper portfolio return and the actual portfolio return in the first analysis.

The component analysis shows not only another way to calculate the implementation shortfall but also the specific components of the shortfall. Thus, residual analysis helps answer such questions as: Are we paying too much in commissions? Are we incurring too high a market impact cost? As it turned out in this example, slippage was the biggest single cost component. The iceberg of trading costs that has been discussed frequently is symbolic of the fact that the mass below the water line, the costs that are not readily visible, is much larger than the mass (the costs) above the water line.[4] The mass under the water is the last two columns of Table 2: slippage ($650) and opportunity costs ($275). Even in this hypothetical example, they account for a large portion of the total implementation shortfall.

Keep in mind that market impact is always measured against the prior night's close. The slippage component indicates the opportunity costs that were initially not counted as part of the realized implementation shortfall. Slippage is measured against the original benchmark because it is a realized opportunity cost, and it also incorporates the impact of the market trend.

Attribution Analysis. Figure 2 illustrates the attribution of the 170 bps in implementation shortfall. By far, the largest portion of the shortfall was a result of slippage (93 bps), which was the realized opportunity costs from delayed trading. The second largest portion of the shortfall was the opportunity costs of the 100 shares (uninvested cash) that remained unexecuted at the end of Day 3. Only 36 bps was a result of market impact, and only 3 bps was a result of commissions.

Figure 2. Implementation Shortfall Attribution

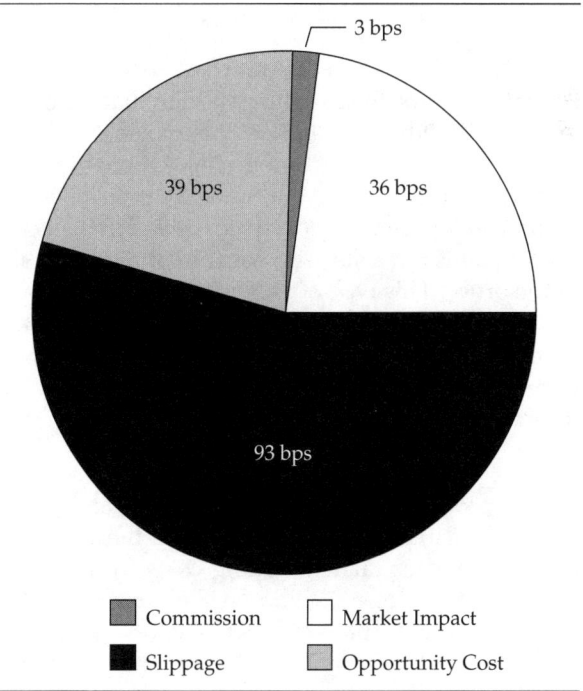

[4]See Figure 1 in Wayne Wagner's workshop presentation "Institutional Order Flow and the Hurdles to Superior Performance" in this proceedings.

The market impact component, the 36 bps, can be broken down even further, as shown in **Figure 3**. Market impact is defined as the difference between the prior night's close and the trade price, but when and at what price the shares in the order are executed can vary throughout the day. The detail of the market impact attribution can clearly show what is hurting the performance of the trade execution.

Figure 3. Market Impact Attribution

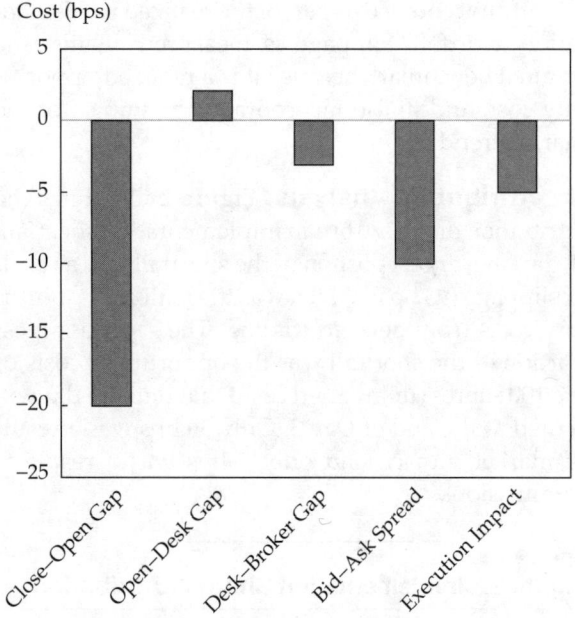

Figure 4. Actual and Expected Total Trading Costs of Buys vs. Sells

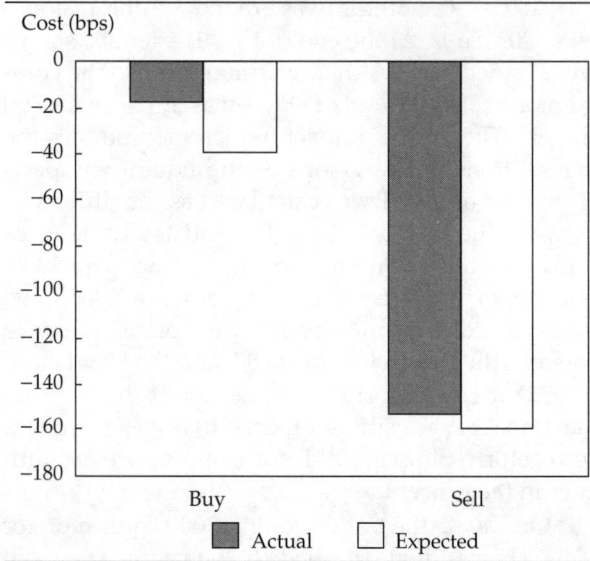

Because the market continues to trade in the overnight hours, the likelihood is high that the close–open gap will be a sizable component of the overall market impact cost, but other components are also important. In this case, the bid–ask spread was the second largest contributor to the market impact cost. This result is not a surprise because of the small size of the order. This type of analysis can be quite informative. In fact, a matrix (e.g., by account, by broker, by trader, by day, by different electronic communications network [ECN]) can be constructed as a tool to analyze quantitatively the source of the market impact trading costs.

Buy vs. Sell Analysis. The last measurement example I will present is an analysis of the difference in actual and estimated trading costs for both buy orders and sell orders, as shown in **Figure 4**. The data for this one example are not based on the trading scenario illustrated in Table 1. The analysis shows that both the actual buy orders and the actual sell orders were executed at a lower cost than estimated by the model used in the rabbit portfolio, and the buys were executed at a relatively lower cost than the sells versus the expected cost. The prevailing market trend will affect the perception of order execution: Execution on buys tends to look good in a declining market, and execution on sells tends to look good in a rising market. The methodology I have used to this point in the presentation does not adjust for this effect. So, some type of adjustment for the market trend needs to be made to accurately assess trading costs.

Figure 5 shows the actual, expected, and market-adjusted trading costs for the same buy and sell transaction illustrated in Figure 4. In the case of the buy order, the market adjustment simply *adds* the amount the market returned over the trading period to the actual trading costs. For example, suppose over the trading period (from inception to execution of the order) for a buy order the market return was a negative 20 bps and the actual trading costs for a buy order were 20 bps. When the market return is added to the actual trading costs, the total market-adjusted cost is then 40 bps, which more closely matches the expected trading costs than at first glance. This adjustment reduces the positive impact of a declining market on the execution of the buy order. In the case of the sell order, the market adjustment *subtracts* the market return over the trading period. Suppose the market return over the trading period was a positive 20 bps. If that return is subtracted from the actual trading costs of the sell order, approximately 155 bps, the total market-adjusted trading costs are reduced to approximately 135 bps. This adjustment reduces the positive impact of a rising market on a sell order. After making the market adjustments, the sells were actually executed at a lower cost relative to the expected cost than the buys were. At this point, further analysis can be done that breaks down each trade by broker, time executed, ECN, and so on.

Figure 5. Market-Adjusted Shortfall for Buys vs. Sells

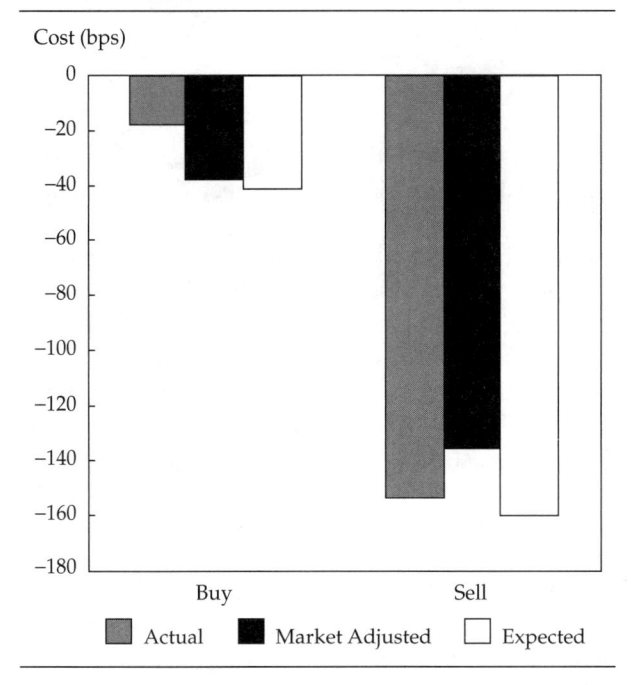

Summary. Many approaches can be used to evaluate the implementation shortfall. The important point is that proper measurement allows the portfolio manager and the trader to know their actual trading costs and where they may be overpaying to trade. In this way, they can learn from their mistakes, and total trading costs can be reduced through managing the six components of trading costs.

Forecasting

Because an optimal trading strategy requires a good forecast of trading costs, forecasting is the second side of the transaction cost management triangle. The reason for managing trading costs is not only to measure the actual trading costs that have been incurred but also to estimate future trading costs so that they can be controlled.

Forecasting Variables. Many different models for forecasting trading costs exist, but each incorporates roughly the same variables. I will briefly discuss the most important of these.

First, the model needs to factor in all sources of liquidity for a stock. For example, Nortel Networks, a Canadian company, is listed on multiple U.S. exchanges and has outstanding American Depositary Receipts. On the one hand, if a particular market or source of liquidity is not typically used by a trader, then the trading costs associated with that market should not be considered in estimating the trading costs for executing an order. On the other hand, suppose substitutes for a stock, such as futures, are often used by a manager to execute a position. In such a case, the cost of using substitutes to achieve the desired liquidity should be considered in estimating trading costs.

Second, the volatility in the market and in a particular stock affects the trading costs of that stock. The higher the level of volatility, the more costly the execution. Third, trading intensity is one of the most important variables that affect the market impact. Think of trading intensity as the size of an order relative to the stock's average liquidity. Other important variables in forecasting trading costs are bid–ask spreads, commissions, and the dependency on certain trading avenues.

In-House vs. Third Party. Although such third-party forecasting models as ITG ACE (Agency Cost Estimator) exist, I believe firms should analyze their trading costs with a method specific to their trading style that incorporates, for example, their manner of broker selection, ECN choice, and so on. Third-party models provide a good reference point, but their trading cost forecasts may be misleading because they are unable to capture the unique trading personality of a firm.

Thus, if a firm has the capital and the know-how, the best way to conduct pretrade and post-trade analysis is with an in-house model that can incorporate all pertinent available information.

Management

The third side of the trade cost management triangle is the ability to consistently manage trading costs. An optimal trading strategy depends on the ability to effectively and quantitatively manage trading costs.

Trade List Generation and Portfolio Optimization. Part of managing trading costs effectively is to incorporate forecasted trading costs into trade list generation and portfolio optimization, which means that trading costs must be forecasted before the trade list is generated. Otherwise, it will be too late to help the portfolio manager maximize the risk-adjusted implementation shortfall or substitute cheaper trades for more expensive trades.

Another aspect of managing trading costs is making sure that the trading team executes orders in a way that is compatible with the model forecast. For example, some trades require immediate execution because the security's alpha value is decaying rapidly. If the trader cannot execute quickly, he or she will lose the ability to trade at an advantageous price and will effectively lose the chance to execute. But in other cases, the trader can wait until the market comes around. The trading team may have the discretion to hold the order over multiple days because the value signal for the stock remains unchanged. When this type of flexibility exists, it should be reflected in the forecasting model.

Because the ultimate goal for the trading and portfolio management teams is to outperform forecasted trading costs, systematic review of actual trading costs and their comparison with estimated trading costs are critical to minimizing the gap between the two.

Quantitative Investment Process. Another way to evaluate trade management is through the quantitative investment process, shown in **Figure 6**. A manager performs research to construct an optimal portfolio using expected return, risk, and transaction costs. Expected trading costs to execute the portfolio manager's strategy have to be considered.

After the portfolio is in place, the manager should conduct an attribution analysis on the portfolio's performance, risk level, and actual execution costs: How much of the performance is driven by alpha, or the manager's skill? How much of the performance is a result of the effectiveness of risk controls? And how much of the performance is generated from skilled trading or the better management of trading costs?

The benefit of quantitative trading cost analysis is the ability to integrate trading costs into the investment process; this approach provides a better chance of achieving best execution. In addition, it is useful in making quantitative broker allocations and in making accurate performance attributions. Therefore, portfolio managers do not have to wait until they "see it" to recognize (or not) best execution.

Execution Score. The following equation is a simplified way to rank brokers based on trading performance:

$$S = 1 - \frac{C}{E(C)},$$

where S is the execution score, C is the implementation shortfall, and $E(C)$ is the expected implementation shortfall.

The first step in the ranking process is to measure the trading costs associated with each broker. This cost is the real implementation shortfall divided by the expected trading costs and takes into account the level of difficulty of a trade. For example, suppose one trade has an expected trading cost of 100 bps, but the actual cost is 90 bps. Suppose another trade has an expected trading cost of 50 bps, but the actual cost is 60 bps. Comparing only the absolute cost of 90 bps versus 60 bps could easily lead to the conclusion that the 60 bp trade is a good trade, or the better trade of the two. But the 90 bp trade actually represents a 10 percent improvement over the expected trading cost, whereas the 60 bp trade represents a 20 percent higher cost than what is expected. The equation provides for relative difficulty in execution so that trading costs can be accurately compared.

An execution score can be assigned to a trader, a trading avenue, a broker, and so on. Using this score simply makes selecting a broker, a trader, a trading avenue, and so on much easier, at least quantitatively. For example, a firm can rank its brokers by this score, using it to give higher allocations to those brokers with the highest scores.

Figure 6. Quantitative Investment Process

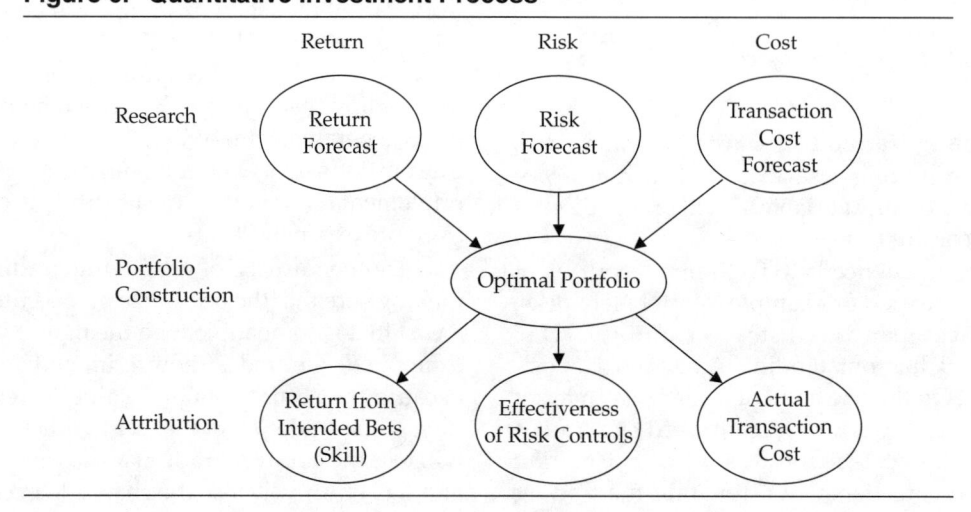

When making this comparison, the firm must remove soft dollars and any other qualitative components from the trades. If a firm is paying 10 cents a share for a trade because it also has a soft-dollar arrangement with the broker, that trade should not be compared with an average trade that is not done under a soft-dollar arrangement. Obviously, the soft-dollar trade will look expensive in comparison.

This quantitative analysis is just a starting point in the broker allocation of orders. Other important questions are how to make the comparison consistent and how to incorporate all of the qualitative and nonquantitative factors involved.

Conclusion

In this presentation, I have advocated the integration of trading and trade cost management into the overall investment and portfolio management process. The process has three components: measurement, forecasting, and management. The measurement stage requires accurate post-trade analysis of the implementation shortfall measured against proper benchmarks. An important factor in the accuracy of trade cost measurement, ignored by many measurement methods, is the need to adjust for the impact that the market trend has on the actual execution of an order. Market trend is not within the control of the trader and thus should not aid or penalize the resulting execution.

Forecasting trading costs is important in trade cost management because it alerts traders and portfolio managers to the expected costs of implementing a particular trading strategy. This information, in turn, allows them to improve realized return by taking trading costs into account as the portfolio is constructed.

Finally, by identifying and understanding trading costs, these costs can be better managed and controlled. Firms can evaluate all the elements in the execution process—traders, trading techniques, brokers, alternative execution venues, and so on—and use the information to achieve best execution.

Question and Answer Session

Minder Cheng

Question: Why measure the market impact cost versus the previous night's close?

Cheng: The term "market impact" has a broad definition, but it can be used narrowly to describe price changes from the time trading is initiated to the time trading concludes. Initiation can mean from the open, the time the trader enters the market, or other points.

Market impact is just one component of transaction costs. The total implementation shortfall is the number that really needs to be tracked. With that in mind, it does not really matter whether you measure market impact against the prior night's close or the open. The important issue is to keep the bigger picture in mind, which is the total implementation shortfall.

Question: Portfolio managers tend to use the price at which they submitted the order (which is often unattainable) as the trade price benchmark. How do you reconcile this issue so that both the manager and the trader are using appropriate benchmarks?

Cheng: In order to achieve best execution, it is imperative to have a two-way conversation between the portfolio management team and the trading team to share both points of view.

Ultimately, it centers on how you incorporate transaction costs into the portfolio management process. If there is no dialogue between the trader and the portfolio manager regarding an order, the portfolio manager has no way of knowing that the trader thinks the manager's benchmark is unrealistic.

Creating that dialogue may involve a redesign or a revamping of your investment organization to ensure that such a dialogue will occur. At Barclays, because we have integrated the portfolio management and trading functions, expected trading costs are automatically incorporated in the portfolio manager's model before he or she begins work each day.

Question: When you adjust costs for the market trend, do you define the market as a specific index or do you use a sector-based adjustment?

Cheng: The adjustment could be as specific as the industry level. The goal is to eliminate the overall market influence, sector influence, industry influence, and so on to find the return that cannot be explained by market forces. But with my example, I wanted to show that even a simple adjustment based on the overall market trend will generally get you to 80 percent of where you want to be.

Question: If you are using your own data to forecast and benchmark your own process's trading costs, isn't it a self-fulfilling outcome?

Cheng: That is a potential problem, so we impose a high standard on the process. Also, to be safe, we involve a third party to assure our investors that we're doing everything appropriately. That is, we benchmark our trades according to our internal procedures and then have a third party independently evaluate and verify the outcome.

Question: How is risk-adjusted implementation shortfall measured?

Cheng: The only way it can be measured is through the portfolio optimization process. If I wanted to minimize the shortfall by 10 bps, it could mean a delayed trade to get that price point. It is important for the optimizer or the portfolio manager to determine an acceptable trade-off between capturing this cost savings versus the risk of delay.

Question: Is VWAP dead, or should it be dead?

Cheng: No, I don't think that VWAP is dead, and I don't think it should be dead. Even though we do not typically use VWAP as a trading benchmark, we do trade VWAP a lot. For orders that can create a large impact on the market at any given instant in time, VWAP can be a good way to spread that impact throughout the day. Even though we are not trading to match or outperform VWAP, embracing VWAP can lead to lower trading costs.

I think that VWAP will be used even more going forward. But it must be used properly. For example, if a firm decides that it is going to benchmark its traders against VWAP, then it must make sure that it measures the difference between last night's close and the VWAP of that day.

Question: The implementation shortfall will be larger for an information or momentum trader than for a value trader, and a market adjustment factor may not adequately reflect trade-specific conditions for individual trades—for example, buying on good news and selling on bad news. Please comment.

Cheng: The reason for making the market adjustment is exactly as the question stated—to differentiate a fast trade, a momentum trade, from one that can wait three days. One way to make this type of adjustment is through expected trading costs, and the other way is through the market adjustment. So, with a fast-moving trade, one in which the portfolio manager is trading on news, I might look at the market return with an adjustment applied to the duration of the trade, which could be 10 seconds, 11 seconds, or 10 days if it is a value trade. By doing this analysis, we hope to eliminate the uncommon factors of trades so that we can fairly compare them.

Views of an "Informed" Trader

Harold S. Bradley
Senior Vice President
American Century Investment Management
Kansas City, Missouri

> The traditional and customary practices of order execution, including the use of soft dollars, are too often in conflict with achieving best execution for investors. Thus, these practices have come under scrutiny by the U.S. SEC and industry standard setters (such as AIMR), and firms have come under pressure to increase trade transparency and improve record keeping and accountability. Among the steps firms should take in this new environment is to demonstrate dedication to reducing trading costs, and among the best tools for that purpose (despite what many in the industry believe) is the electronic communications network.

As a former trader and portfolio manager at American Century Investment Management (ACIM), I have observed firsthand the difficulties involved in trading and the achievement of best execution. In particular, I have noticed how much of the investment management business uses the trading desk as a bill-paying function to support the business enterprise rather than as a mechanism for carrying out the fiduciary obligations owed to the client to provide best execution and to maximize the value of investment decisions. In this presentation, I will discuss the problems that stem from the myriad cross-subsidies that have been built into the commission stream and discuss how the current research payment systems may be subject to regulatory scrutiny and reform.

What Is Best Execution?

A definition of best execution appears just about everywhere: due diligence manuals, marketing presentations, consultant questionnaires, and requests for proposals. No legal definition exists, however, or at least traditionally, there has not been one. Thus, the search for best execution has proven elusive, despite the many assurances otherwise. "We know it when we see it, but it is really hard to measure," is an oft-quoted expression on trading desks when alluding to the concept of best execution. Traders are not paid to make decisions that really work to achieve best execution and have disincentives to doing so: They have soft-dollar chits to pay and shares waiting to trade for impatient, demanding, and often unrealistic portfolio managers. Traders operate under what I call "maximum risk aversion for maximum pay on the desk." As a portfolio manager, when I made a bad decision, I blamed the trading desk. Trading is a function in which it is difficult to claim "value added" and easy to look bad in a handful of trades. As a result, it is no surprise that traders give the ambivalent answers they do when asked about best execution.

New Definition. In 2000, before leaving the U.S. SEC, former commissioner Arthur Levitt started the process of articulating new standards for best execution. At the same time, both the Investment Company Institute (ICI) and AIMR were asked to convene best practices groups to help define best execution. At the December 2000 ICI Securities Law Development Conference, Gene Gohlke, associate director of the SEC Office of Compliance Inspections and Examinations, offered this definition of best execution:

> In placing a trade, the trading desk will seek to find a broker/dealer or alternative trading system that will execute a trade in a way that the trader believes will realize the maximum value of the investment decision.

Given the conventional wisdom surrounding best execution, this definition presents a challenge to the industry.

Editor's note: This presentation is reprinted from the AIMR proceedings *Best Execution and Portfolio Performance* (Charlottesville, VA: AIMR, 2001).

The "investment decision" referred to in Gohlke's definition pertains to the particular trade being executed—not to Goldman Sachs' research yesterday, First Boston's research last week, or a consultant who directs a lot of business to the firm. In terms of words, the change is minor, but in terms of policy, the change is rather substantial. And the addition of "alternative trading systems" in the definition is a big change. The use of electronic communications networks (ECNs) and nontraditional trading systems has exploded in the market in the past 10 years. Yet, I am told that on the buy side, institutional money managers still directly use these systems less than 7–8 percent of the time.

In his presentation, Gohlke identified possible areas in which SEC auditors will spend more time. Note that he was not talking to investment professionals but, rather, to the lawyers who advise the outside directors who, in turn, advise funds and money managers. Investment managers have fiduciary obligations to boards as well as to investors in the areas of compliance systems, compliance evaluation procedures, and record keeping. Accordingly, the SEC is saying that the hiring of a consultant to measure execution quality is not sufficient proof that a manager is in compliance with getting best execution; the adequacy of order-handling systems, trade-error experience, and timeliness of execution reports will be reviewed; and the allotment of initial public offering (IPO) shares against requested allocations will be assessed.

Basically, the SEC appears to have serious concerns about how Section 28(e) of the Securities Exchange Act of 1934, which provides a "safe harbor" for firms to pay up for research, has been used and interpreted. In addition, the use of ECNs—as venues that provide greater liquidity, price improvement, and lower commission rates—will be evaluated. Many people on the buy side are not using ECNs, and this new mandate from the SEC means that the regulators want to know why.

AIMR Trade Management Guidelines. AIMR's proposed Trade Management Guidelines on best execution were announced in November 2001.[1] The AIMR recommendations are consistent with the direction of the SEC. The guidelines recommend the establishment of trade management oversight committees that will be responsible for developing a trade management policy and a process to manage the efficacy of trades. Are you getting what you are paying for? Are you evaluating the service you received? And are you evaluating the providers of that service?

Specifically, the implications of these guidelines are as follows:

- Substantial infrastructure spending will occur to build record-keeping and reporting systems to track and audit trading information appropriately because so many firms still operate with inadequate order management systems.
- The negotiation of acceptable commission ranges and documentation of the variance between negotiated and actual commission rates will become necessary. Commission rates that held at 5–6 cents a share for more than a decade should and will be negotiated down to a level closer to the 1.00–1.25 cents a share rate paid on ECNs for execution-only services.
- Trade management oversight committees will be established, and the internal documents prepared for these committees will be auditable by the SEC. The SEC has already been asking for these materials.
- Real and potential conflicts of interest must be documented.
- The choice of a particular trading system must be supported, and the review and evaluation of trades, broker selection, and execution performance can be expected.

What Are Soft Dollars Really Buying?

In Gohlke's definition of best execution, traders are charged with maximizing the value of the trade decision. But Robert Schwartz, the Marvin M. Speiser Professor of Finance at Baruch College, City University of New York, and Benn Steil, at the Council of Foreign Investors, have studied how little control traders actually have over the execution decision. They sent questionnaires to the chief investment officers of major investment companies that asked, "Who at your firm controls institutional commission payments?" They found that 62 percent of all trades are not controlled by traders.[2] (This finding is consistent with my experience as a trader and portfolio manager.) The report also addresses how often commissions are used to pay for things other than best execution. And Steil, aggregating the information from a variety of reports on commission bundling, has stated that nearly two-thirds of soft-dollar agreements

---

[1] Since the writing of this presentation, the final guidelines have been issued. They can be accessed at www.aimr.org/pdf/standards/ trademgmt_guidelines.pdf.

[2] Robert Schwartz and Benn Steil, "Controlling Institutional Trading Costs," *Journal of Portfolio Management* (Spring 2002):39–49.

are unwritten and more than one-third of brokers are a party to illegal soft-dollar arrangements.[3]

Clearly, soft-dollar agreements play an important role in the execution decision and are often in direct conflict with an investment firm's fiduciary duty to the client. What are soft dollars really buying? How extensively is soft-dollar business affecting the trading decision and ultimately usurping the goal of best execution?

Research. Investment managers pay up for execution and have a safe harbor to do so to some extent under Section 28(e), because in exchange for paying up, they receive company proprietary research services, including access to analysts and road shows with corporate executives. But now that these executives are subject to Regulation Fair Disclosure (FD), why are managers still willing to pay up?

The willingness to pay up is especially thought-provoking because most investment management firms choose to "buy" their research from brand-name companies (paying up relatively more), even when firm or brand name is obviously not a proxy for quality. Based on the following observations, this attraction to brand appears to be quite misplaced: Only 41 percent of analysts at the 10 largest brokers (what I consider the brand-name brokers) rank as StarMine four- or five-star analysts, compared with 35 percent of analysts at all firms having 10 or more analysts.[4] Rankings are based on the earliest directional correctness and accuracy of the analysts' EPS estimates for the trailing four quarters and two years as well as on the accuracy of buy, sell, and hold recommendations. The top five firms with the largest percentage of four- and five-star analysts are regional or niche research firms without significant investment banking activities, namely, Buckingham Research Group, Gerard Klauer Mattison, Pacific Growth Equities, U.S. Bancorp, and WR Hambrecht + Company. At the 10 largest brokers, 25 percent of the analysts ranked poorly, as one- or two-star performers. Obviously, the rationale that brand-name research is a worthy use of the client's commission dollar is suspect at best. Yet, the industry persists in supporting the practice of "buying" research with soft dollars, which is a major factor in holding negotiated commission rates at the 6 cent level.

■ *A safe harbor?* In his speech to the Securities Industry Association in November 2000, Levitt asked whether portfolio managers were bringing to bear the pressure they should on brokerage commission rates and why the emergence of electronic markets had not driven full-service commissions lower. If a trade on an ECN costs a penny or less a share, why do most people on the buy side still pay 5–6 cents a share? Do portfolio managers and independent directors think 6 cents is safe, that it falls within the safe harbor exception of Section 28(e)?

Levitt said that 6 cents is not a safe rate and that those who think it is should reexamine the part of their business that is predicated on 6 cents being safe. The status quo of the industry's trading and execution practices is being seriously challenged by the SEC. And **Figure 1** shows that, although the median commission rate has been steadily decreasing since 1989 because of technological advances and commission unbundling, immediately following Levitt's speech in 2000, the median rate dropped below 5 cents a share. Apparently, the market heard and understood the message.

■ *The real cost of research.* Understandably, investors must pay a cost for block trading, capital facilitation, value-added research, and IPOs, but what is that cost (i.e., the real cost of trading)? **Figure 2** compares average cost-per-share rates at ACIM with the industry median. The solid line depicts the rates our agency brokers have been willing to negotiate. The rate has not dropped significantly since 1989, even though we have tried, with minimal success, to move it lower. (Of course, with regulators and professional organizations like AIMR and ICI moving the issues of best execution and soft-dollar business to the forefront, the tenor and tone of the market changed markedly in 2001.)

The dashed line in Figure 2 shows ACIM's average cost for using ECNs, where we do 35–40 percent of our business. The difference in the rate charged by our agency brokers and the rate charged by the ECNs can be thought of as a premium paid for research. In 2001, this premium is at an all-time high. When the value of research should be worth far less than ever before, given Regulation FD and the information overload via the Internet, the cost of soft-dollar research is at a record high mainly because technology has lowered the *real* cost of trading while the "old rules" of trading and execution have kept the actual cost of trading artificially high.

I used to be convinced that the more business we did on ECNs, the more our costs would rise (and the less the marginal benefit would be) because of a structural reversion to the mean. **Table 1** illustrates, however, that the mean for all-in trading costs is down, not up. As our business on these nontraditional systems increases, our overall efficacy, as measured against other brokers doing similar business in the

---

[3] Benn Steil, "Can Best Execution Be Achieved in the Current Market Structure?" Presentation given at the AIMR conference "Improving Portfolio Performance through Best Execution," November 30–December 1, 2000, Chicago.

[4] StarMine is an ACIM portfolio company.

Figure 1. NYSE-Listed Share Trading Volume and Capital Research Associates' Industry Median Commissions, 1989–2001

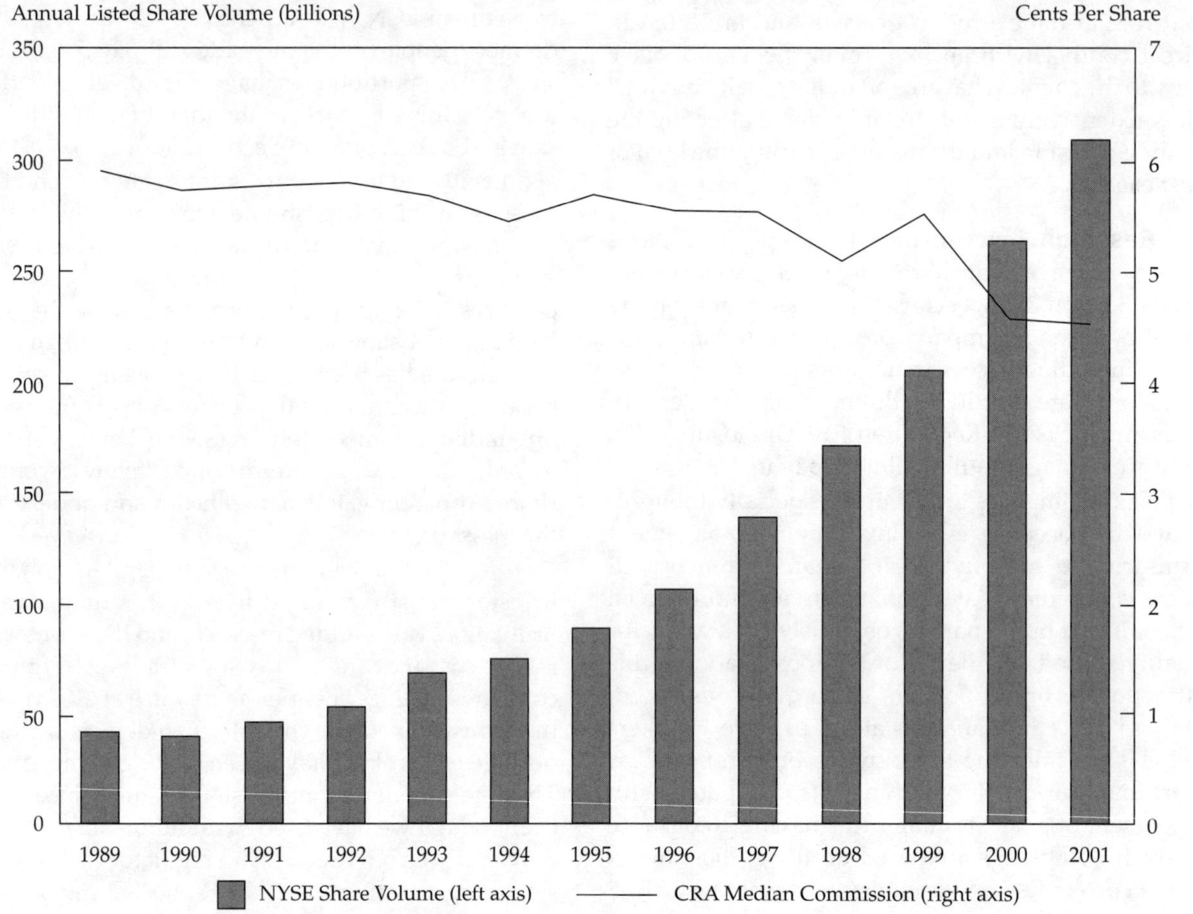

Note: Commission chart inclusive of ECN agency fees.

same time frame, has widened. ECNs are far more effective than the traditional exchanges. They remove structural, intermediated costs.

The nontraditional players, highlighted in bold in Table 1, are important; in particular, B-Trade, Archipelago, and Instinet have helped lower our costs of trading. Broker 3, one of the most respected Nasdaq market-making firms in the business, produced costs equal to 2.03 percent of principal, round-trip on Nasdaq trades, whereas Archipelago and Instinet both produced a negative cost. According to Capital Research Associates' methodology, "negative cost" means that the day after our order is finished, the price of the stock we sold is still falling. In other words, we have not telegraphed our intentions to the rest of the market in moving big orders and we have succeeded in executing at a relatively fair price.

Use of electronic trading for listed stocks has only recently begun to pick up steam; Archipelago linked into the Nasdaq system to display orders in the public market early in 2001. Traders can now put their order indications into the public quote system and split the spreads charged by the specialists. The ability to lower costs this way is compelling.

Market Stability. For decades, brokers have justified all types of structural cross-subsidies by claiming that when markets are under stress, the broker will help stabilize the market. The popular theory was that the ability to get best execution depends on a broker's willingness to lay capital on the line during times of market distress, when that capital infusion is really needed.

In their article, Schwartz and Steil conclude, instead, that the buy-side institutions' call on street capital for immediacy of execution is an insurance or option to protect the investment manager's identity and order size from being captured by intermediaries and transmitted to competitors—to avoid being

Figure 2. Historical Commission Trends, 1989–2001

Average Cost Per Share (cents)

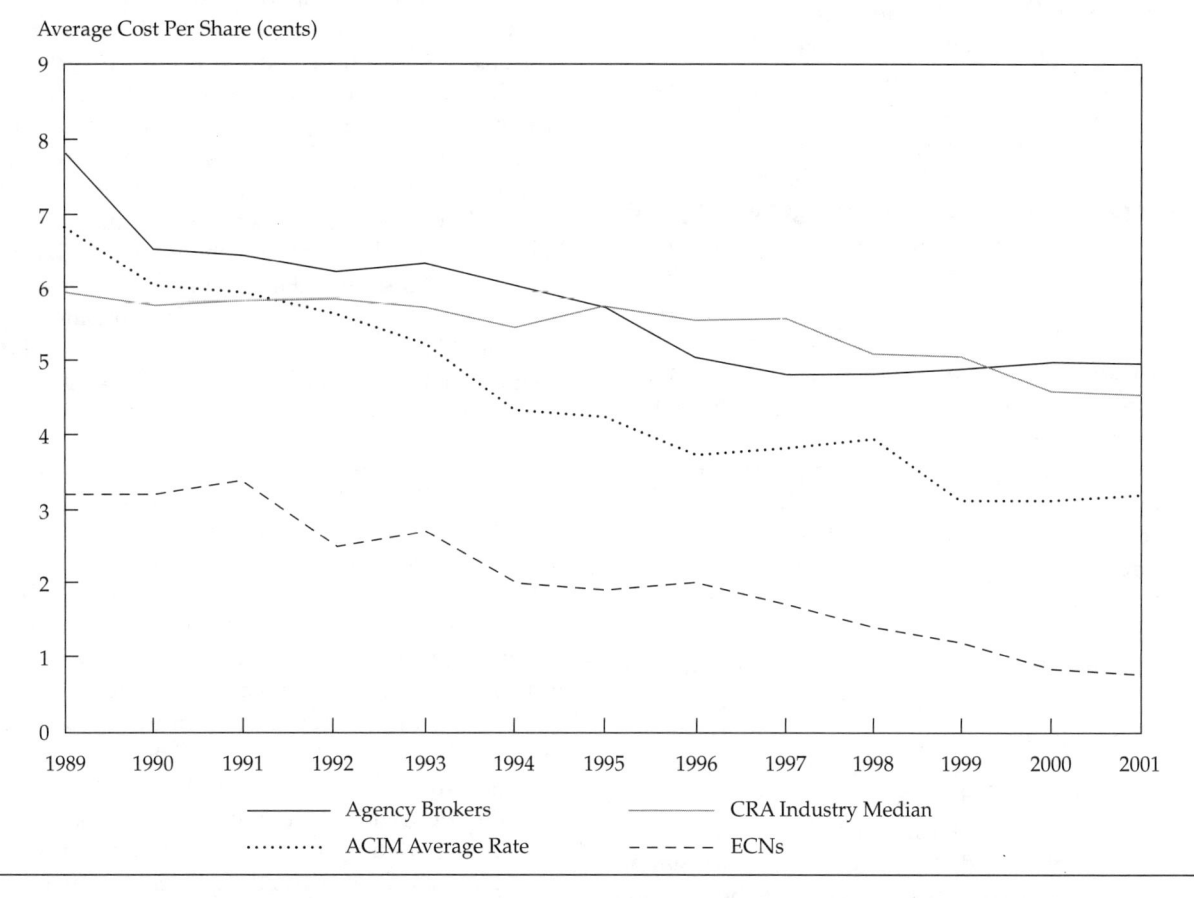

— Agency Brokers
— CRA Industry Median
······· ACIM Average Rate
– – – ECNs

Table 1. Capital Research Associates' Study of ACIM All-In Trading Costs

Broker	Dollars Traded	Average Market Cap (billions)	Average Volatility	Cost as Percentage of Principal OTC	Cost as Percentage of Principal Listed
ACIM funds average	$47,607,820,875	$56.76	51%	0.49 bps	0.32 bps
Broker 1	4,263,056,375	48.67	45	0.66	0.28
Broker 2	2,637,630,000	47.28	45	0.93	0.23
Broker 3	1,672,943,750	42.69	56	2.03	–0.40
Broker 4[a]	1,738,325,000	35.23	51	–1.00	0.24
Instinet	2,219,195,000	61.35	61	–0.23	–2.72
Crossing Network	923,983,750	45.17	53	0.61	–0.25
B-Trade	3,697,211,250	56.24	63	0.84	–0.28
Archipelago	5,855,745,250	65.83	64	–0.06	–0.46
Traditional brokers[b]	10,311,955,125	43.47	49	0.66	0.09
Electronic brokers	12,696,135,250	57.15	60	0.29	–0.93

Note: Data reflect non-dollar-weighted mean of 10 six-month periods, June 30, 1997, through June 30, 2001 (post-order-handling rules).

[a]Negative OTC costs are a function of aftermarket IPO performance.
[b]The "traditional brokers" category reflects four large brokers only.

front-run. To support their contention, Schwartz and Steil point out that, based on the responses to their survey, portfolio managers only rarely create orders based on seeing the other side through a telephone call, trading activity, or order flow in the market. Investment managers appear to be attributing their willingness to pay up for liquidity to a reason that is not borne out in practice.

Order Life Cycle

Understanding how orders are executed and how the trading system is changing can shed light on the challenges of achieving best execution because of competing interests in the trading process. The life cycle of an order at the NYSE follows a convoluted route littered with at least seven intermediaries: An order travels from a portfolio manager to the trader, to a broker sales trader, to a "block," "position," or "upstairs" trader, to a floor broker, and finally, to the specialist post. Here is how it works. A portfolio manager decides to buy a stock and calls his institutional trader at the trading desk. That trader then tries to figure out which broker she might have heard from in the last two days that might have an order in that stock or, as likely, identifies a broker to whom the manager owes a consultant bill or who holds a soft-dollar chit. She then gives the trade to the trader at that brokerage firm. The broker sales trader is the most frequent and trusted point of contact for the institutional sales trader.

But then there is the broker "upstairs" trader, whose job is to trade the firm's block capital. The reason brokers staff a sales trader position is ostensibly to protect the investor from the upstairs trader. For example, if the investor gives a 500,000-share order to the sales trader in Chicago, a trusted sales trader will not immediately disclose this information to the upstairs trader in New York. If the upstairs trader communicates this information throughout the system and is then asked to bid someone else's stock, that information alone might trigger "go along" activity and have an unfavorable impact on the price of the first trader's order. Investors need protection from the upstairs trader, but that upstairs trader is also the broker's representative for the investor's interest with the NYSE floor broker. The floor broker may be representing not only the firm representing that investor but also other firms and, therefore, other investors. The floor broker then goes to the specialist, who posts the order to the tape as part of the National Best Bid and Offer (NBBO) system, as seen on Bloomberg. The whole process is repeated on the other side of the trade.

Now consider order half-life. Orders travel from investor to specialist, with successively smaller order amounts passing from trader to trader within this sort of "bucket brigade." Everybody buys and sells exactly the same way. After an investor gives the institutional trader 500,000 shares to trade, that institutional trader gives the sales trader 250,000 shares to trade. The sales trader gives the upstairs trader 125,000 shares to trade, and the upstairs trader, through the floor broker, tells the specialist to post 25,000 shares. With such a system, no wonder traders believe that trading is a win–lose function.

In a market driven by eighths (before decimalization), commissions and trading spreads were plentiful and the mix of traditional roles in the execution process was sufficient assurance that everyone on the sell side would do well. In a market now driven by decimals, the life cycle of an order has not changed but the economics of the business certainly has. In the retail universe, a theory exists that payment for order flow and internalization of orders has been a large part of the profits of the business. This precedent is collapsing because both ECNs and decimalization have so markedly changed the economics of the execution process.

The Specialist. Because of the completely counterintuitive auction rules that govern trading on the NYSE, getting the best price in the market is often difficult. Let me explain what I mean with the following example. Say I go to a wine auction to buy a special case of wine. I want this wine badly because it is rated as one of the top wines of the new vintages; in 10 years, it will be worth a bundle, plus I will have good wine in the cellar. The bidding starts and quickly rises to $3,000 a bottle. I know I should not pay that much, but the auctioneer calls the bid and says I just purchased the wine. The case is opened, and I am handed four bottles—and then four bottles go to a person who was sitting three feet away from me who never opened her mouth, and another four bottles go to someone on the telephone. Before the bidding started and unknown to me, these two people said that they wanted to participate in the trade and buy at the highest price that cleared the supply.

Such are the rules of trading at the NYSE. The rules allow free options to third parties, so despite the theory published in the academic literature on auction markets, serious obstacles exist to discovering an appropriate clearing price. As long as a third party is allowed to forgo the risk of price discovery, that third party gets a free option on whatever is being traded. I find that situation fundamentally wrong. In my earlier example, the wine seller did not get the right price because I, as an interested buyer, was not allowed to bid for all the bottles I wanted and the other bidders were essentially removed from the bidding process altogether.

Little information is available on the profitability of specialists. A major NYSE specialist firm, LaBranche & Company, did recently go public, however, which provided some clues. The initial offering prospectus showed that LaBranche consistently earned more than 75 percent of its profits from dealer trader activity, had been profitable every quarter for 22 years, and averaged consistent returns on capital and equity of more than 70 percent. If LaBranche's numbers are typical of the economics of NYSE specialists, are investors benefiting from the intervention of the specialist, or do specialists simply impose another layer of expense?

Clean Cross Rule. The clean cross rule (Rule 72[b]) at the NYSE also grants a free option for liquidity takers and proprietary interests. A clean cross is a trade involving a matched pair of buy and sell orders of 25,000 shares or more that cannot be broken up (that is, disclosed floor interest is not included in the trade). Rule 72(b) currently gives priority to clean crosses at or within the prevailing quotation, and crosses are not allowed if any part of the cross is an order for the account of a member or member firm. An amendment to Rule 72(b) filed by the NYSE provides for clean crosses even if all or part of the order is for a member or member firm. Say you are a buyer bidding for 25,000 shares at $20 and the order is on the book as a limit order displayed for the whole world to see on Bloomberg. A broker has a customer who wants to sell 100,000 shares at $20 and another customer (or the broker himself) who wants to buy 100,000 at $20. They trade with each other, and your order remains unexecuted. Such a situation is worse than the situation with the specialist I just described because under the amendment, a broker can trade proprietarily on one side of a block trade and ignore preexisting orders on the trading floor.

The rules of trading are designed for the intermediaries and grant absolute free options to limit order traders in the market. Transparent limit orders provide the basis for price discovery in listed equities markets. I believe limit orders are an endangered species.

Institutional Xpress. The NYSE has finally paid attention to the ICI, which has been saying for a long time that limit orders are being subjected to free options. Accordingly, the NYSE established Institutional Xpress, which is designed to allow the institutional investor to take an offering or hit a displayed limit order through the NYSE DOT (designated order turnaround) system without an attempt to gain price improvement. Ironically, the rules governing Institutional Xpress provide an opportunity for, instead, price improvement of a market order. This is but another example of rules beneficial to brokers and inimical to the interests of buy-side traders.

Why *Not* ECNs?

ECNs improve the traditional execution mechanism and eliminate the requirement of dealing with the specialist. An ECN is a limit order book, and limit orders have primacy. The most important aspects of primacy are price priority, time priority, anonymity, and an order cancellation privilege—absolute control over entry into and exit from the market. The ability to cancel orders at will establishes a potential time value on options; they are no longer free. Nicholas Economides and Schwartz found that investors appreciate the motives for trading on ECNs but that the soft-dollar arrangements that traders must satisfy may stymie ECN use.[5]

Nevertheless, despite the electronic trading systems' proven advantages, the buy side still has not welcomed ECNs with open arms. Ian Domowitz and Steil concluded:

> An examination of total trading costs, inclusive of commissions, reveals electronic trading to be superior to traditional brokerage by any measure of trade difficulty for buy trades and to be comparable for sells.[6]

Traders give several reasons for not trading on ECNs. Traders claim that large orders cannot be executed efficiently on ECNs and that executing through ECNs conflicts with the immediacy required to execute before an anticipated market move. Traders need to recognize that, in fact, ECNs not only offer the anonymity they seek but can also effectively execute large orders through rapid-fire small, block-equivalent trades—as do brokers and market makers today.

Anonymity. Above all, both buy-side *and* sell-side traders seek order anonymity in the market. Yet, the identity of the firm, the size of the firm, and its trading practices are all known by the intermediary chosen to execute an order for a buy-side client. That intermediary has a relationship with at least 200 other high-commission-paying firms. Certainly, a relationship with some degree of trust exists between the trader and the sales trader, but that trust can break down rather easily. Because of the very nature of the system, then, believing that a firm is working just for you or not leaking information about your order into the system is naive. ECNs, however, are the very definition of anonymity in trading.

Size. Traders have been heard to say, "Look at these screens. The orders are all for 1,000 shares, and on Nasdaq, they are offering 100 shares; there is no

---

[5] Nicholas Economides and Robert A. Schwartz, "Equity Trading Practices and Market Structure: Assessing Asset Managers' Demand for Immediacy," *Financial Markets, Institutions & Instruments* (November 1995):1–45.

[6] Ian Domowitz and Benn Steil, "Automation, Trading Costs, and the Structure of the Securities Trading Industry," *Brookings-Wharton: Papers on Financial Services*, edited by Robert E. Litan and Anthony M. Santomero (Washington, DC: The Brookings Institution, 1999):33–81.

liquidity." This liquidity argument is largely moot; large, hidden limit orders, which are basically reserve quantities, exist on ECNs. The Nasdaq has just petitioned for a rule change that would allow market makers to show only 100 shares of an order to the market while at the same time placing as much as tens of thousands of shares in a nontransparent order queue. A benefit of this capability is that to trade 1,000 shares, you can execute 10 trades of 100 shares electronically and virtually simultaneously without advertising to adversaries what you are doing.

Buy-side traders prefer to trade large blocks of stock because blocks are easier to account for and to book. The typical trader's viewpoint is that block trades cannot be executed on ECNs. But we find that when we use an ECN for listed trades and an order is published and highly visible, we tend to attract the other side of an order more easily. That advantage has interesting implications, especially considering the recent merger between Archipelago and REDI-Book and the SEC's approval of Archipelago becoming a fully electronic exchange. With the emergence of a fully electronic exchange, the buy side will apparently be able to drive the best price in the market while avoiding unnecessary intermediation.

A block trade that uses a broker's capital is not a charitable gift. Brokers traditionally "rent" capital when trading a block because natural counterparties are said to occur only about 20 percent of the time. Brokers regularly make capital for block facilitation available only to payers of the largest commissions—which is functionally identical to offering a commission discount. Then, if they lose money on the trades, they earn full "rents" from smaller full-commission players, so they are making up the difference with commissions from the smaller firms that do not have that same kind of leverage with the broker. This "loss ratio" is a major component of the cross-subsidies that underpin the soft-dollar business. Ultimately, the little guy loses.

Historically, brokers served as "small order aggregators" working off negotiated block transactions in small increments over the phone, SelectNet, or ECNs. ECNs, however, eliminate the risk premium that institutions pay to trade; technology replaces capital in the aggregation process.

Our traders work aggressively to get the best price for block size on ECNs. At ACIM, we use FIX technology, the Financial Information Exchange protocol, to send orders to ECNs, and we have been successful in trading extremely large orders on ECNs; we regularly execute orders of more than a million shares. Surprisingly, the average trade size for a Nasdaq stock on an ECN is fewer than 1,000 shares. We use DOT and Archipelago to access the liquidity on the NYSE, and we are increasingly successful at trading large orders in NYSE-listed securities on ECNs.

A good example of our success in trading blocks on ECNs is what we were able to accomplish during the period from 1 June to 31 August 2001, the summer doldrums, when the entire equity market's volume is at its lowest level. We averaged on a daily basis more than 13 orders of more than 50,000 shares; 6 orders between 50,000 and 100,000 shares; 4 orders between 101,000 and 250,000 shares; and almost 2 orders between 251,000 and 500,000 shares. And these trade sizes are fairly conservative in terms of what can be executed on ECNs. For example, during the same period, we used ECNs to trade 12.1 million shares of AOL with an average order size of 202,000 shares and a total principal value of $526 million. We also traded 12.1 million shares of Pfizer ($494 million of principal and average order size of 181,000 shares).

We chose to make these trades on ECNs because we wanted anonymity. When the market sees you trading in a name, the other buyers immediately look to see how big you are in the name and make inferences about why you are selling or buying. That is how the Street anticipates price action.

Immediacy. Another buy-side trader objection to using ECNs is the need to implement a trade "right now" in one block at a single price. Part of the trader's demand for immediacy is the culture of blame transfer—that is, portfolio managers blaming traders for the portfolio managers' own mistakes. When the buy-side trader hands an order to a broker, the trader has someone to yell at on behalf of an impatient portfolio manager.

Schwartz and Steil surveyed portfolio managers and chief investment officers about how much weight they give in stock purchase decisions to an estimate of share price in one day, one week, one quarter, one year, or two years or more. Most managers profess that they do not care what the share price will be one day or even one quarter out but do care about the price at one to two years out. That finding has profound implications. Why would portfolio managers, who may take days or weeks to make a purchase or sell decision, expect a trade to be done "right now" unless their ego is heavily invested in micromanaging the trader? Schwartz and Steil also asked how soon the managers expected a price correction to occur when buying or selling a stock that was believed to be mispriced. Most answered one month to one year or more than one year, not less than an hour or one week to one month. So, again, managers' timing expectations do not appear to align with their demands. Immediacy is simply not the impetus for trading that many managers claim.

Changes Affecting ECNs

In 1975, the Exchange Act called for a linked national market in which prices in one market would be respected in other markets. More than 20 years passed before the SEC took another major step toward encouraging market linkage with the enactment of the order-handling rules in 1997. These rules were an attempt to tie together markets fragmented by Instinet and other ECNs. It required ECNs to include orders in the public display of the NBBO. Although the Nasdaq intermarket gives ECNs a path to the listed market and exchange-traded funds, barriers to unification of the markets exist, such as the access fee the ECNs are charged. Archipelago chose to voluntarily comply with the order-handling rules but is the only ECN to have done so. The SEC has suggested that the application of the order-handling rules and Regulation ATS (alternative trading systems) to listed stocks is unfinished business. ECNs, however, represent an estimated 40 percent of Nasdaq volume, and ECN quotes drive the inside market.

The intermarket trading system (ITS)/Computer Assisted Execution System (CAES) link to the NBBO offered by Nasdaq to its members, who include Archipelago, is rapidly changing the marketplace. For the 62 days ending 31 March 2001, before Archipelago linked to the market through ITS/CAES, we traded only 35 orders for NYSE-listed stocks, compared with 121 listed orders in the 65 days after the linkage on 31 August 2001. Pre-ITS/CAES, these orders were excluded from market quotes, but post-ITS/CAES, the orders were transparent as limit orders to all market participants. We can now advertise our intention to trade.

Nevertheless, some traders are expressing frustrations similar to those expressed about Nasdaq trades before the instigation of the order-handling rules. The complaint is about "trade-throughs" and "backing away" (the latter occurs when one linked market trades at an inferior price to another market's price—say, the NYSE— as reflected in the NBBO). We started putting our listed orders into the system, and because of trade-throughs, we could not get some trades executed without compromise. As a result, Archipelago and Nasdaq built so-called "whiner" software (because we whined a lot). The "whine" is automatically triggered when (1) the public quote exceeds 100 shares at a price in the NBBO and (2) the order in Archipelago's ARCA book is at a superior price to the competing exchange and (3) the ARCA order is displayed for 15 seconds before a trade takes place at the inferior price in the NYSE and (4) the trade remains unexecuted for at least 10 seconds after the trade at the inferior price.

Whining is a frequent occurrence. The specialists believe the market resides with them, and an imputed belief is that the regional exchanges are not contributing to price discovery, which has, in fact, been true historically. Prior to decimalization, the regional exchanges were used primarily by retail firms, such as Charles Schwab & Company, to maximize profitability by routing orders and earning payment for order flow from the regional exchanges.

Since decimalization, the practice of payment for order flow appears to be breaking down, which has changed the economic structure of many order flow arrangements. Now, as real electronic orders flow through Nasdaq (and soon, through the Pacific Coast Exchange), the NYSE is trying to make sure orders have to come to it. A good audit trail does not exist that reveals the primary exchanges' failure to recognize better prices on regional exchanges. But from mid-June through August, Archipelago and Nasdaq recorded more than 1,500 NYSE whines a day, which is a big concern. It means that either the specialists cannot keep up with both an electronic market and a physical market, which is a reasonable explanation, or that they are ignoring the electronic market because they are granting free options to the floor crowd.

Until the market adjusts to a more integrated system, these whines have important implications for how managers manage, especially given the environment of 2–4 percent real expected stock returns suggested by Robert Arnott and Peter Bernstein[7] and the fact that the cost of trading is estimated to be 1–3 percent for small- and mid-cap stocks.

The impediments to trading are regulatory—that is, driven by market regulations designed to protect the owners of the marketplace. I am a big fan of Archipelago's move to partner with the Pacific Stock Exchange to form a new for-profit stock exchange. A for-profit stock exchange is not owned by intermediaries and not run for intermediaries; it is owned by and run for the stockholders.

Conclusion

The problems with achieving best execution cannot be separated from the existing economics of trading systems and the reluctance of traders and portfolio managers to change the way they approach the trading function. Roughly 65 percent of ECN users are broker/dealers and hedge funds and 25 percent are day traders. As I mentioned earlier, only about 7–8 percent of ECN users are on the buy side. Schwartz and Steil wrote:

---

[7] Robert D. Arnott and Peter L. Bernstein, "What Risk Premium Is 'Normal'?" *Financial Analysts Journal* (March/April 2002):64–85.

Survey results clearly suggest that the traditional explanation for immediacy demand . . . is overstated. We conclude that the buy side's demand for immediacy is in appreciable part endogenous to an intermediated environment that is characterized by front-running.

Although some may find this view to be too cynical, the statement summarizes the behavior and rationale that I have witnessed over the course of my career.

Is unbundling of commissions and research and other soft-dollar services desirable and feasible? In the same Schwartz and Steil survey mentioned previously, they found that 51 percent of managers believe unbundling commissions from the research process is desirable and only 8 percent believe it is undesirable. The bundled process, however, has a major positive impact on the earnings stream of many investment managers.

In the United Kingdom, Paul Myners, chairman of the Gartmore Group and one of the most respected money managers in the United Kingdom, was asked to investigate the inefficiencies of capital formation for small- and mid-cap U.K. firms. One of the recommendations he made was that all commissions be paid by the manager out of the management fee.[8] U.K. firms have been given two years to respond to and implement the recommendations.

Although such action is a long way off in the United States, in light of the SEC's direction and AIMR's new guidelines, U.S. firms should begin to address the following questions:

- Is the commission you pay really protected by the safe harbor? It probably is not safe at 6 cents, or even 5 cents.
- Do you use ECNs? When? How much? How do you make that choice? You must first give your traders permission to be traders.
- Do you pay the same brokerage rate to all vendors and the same rate on all trades? If so, why? Lower negotiated rates alone are not sufficient. The SEC is looking for some variance within the rates paid to the same broker among trades. Some firms are paying 2–3 cents for taking the other side of a trade and paying 6 cents for capital commitment. These investment management firms have a formula for determining what they pay for various kinds of trades.
- How do you measure best execution? Whether you use Capital Research Associates, Plexus Group (implementation shortfall methodology), or volume-weighted average price, part of the answer to achieving best execution lies in having a process to measure it.
- Have you invested in sufficient trading technology? Or are your traders bill-paying order clerks?
- Do you know where your orders go? The order execution process is, in my opinion, sausage making at its worst. It is where the source of performance resides, especially in a potentially low-return environment.
- Regarding step-outs, are the rates and best execution promises consistent with what your marketing agent tells the sponsor? A lot of firms use step-outs and think they are getting best execution by using them. But almost everybody I talk to on the sell side tells me they have an A list and a B list, and the firms that step out are on the B list. If you are calling a potential buyer with merchandise and you know there are three or four buyers around and you have a seller for something that is hot, you call the buyer that will maximize your income. You cannot maximize your income on that trade if 40 percent of the trade is going to be stepped out to a third party.

Attention to these issues will help firms get on the right track and avoid problems in the future.

The bottom line is that trading decisions are not driven simply by the search for best execution. Too many conflicting economic currents and motivations affect the execution decision, which more often than not, is made by someone other than the trader. Paying up to execute is a function of the traditional and customary practice of buying broker services—research and market stability—with soft dollars, but this practice has been targeted by the SEC and industry standard setters (such as AIMR) as needing increased transparency and improved record keeping and accountability.

---

[8]See Marcus Hooper's presentation in this proceedings.

Cost versus Liquidity: The Quest for Best Execution

Wayne H. Wagner
Co-Founder and Chairman
Plexus Group, Inc.
Los Angeles

> The trading process that begins with a portfolio manager decision demands a trade-off decision by the trader: "Do I focus on cost or on liquidity?" The answer to this balancing act is part of the larger issue of best execution, which has been addressed by many organizations—from the U.S. SEC to AIMR. AIMR's Trade Management Guidelines get best execution right, in principle, but fall short in other areas.

Cost versus liquidity: That is the trader's dilemma. Traders must ask themselves: "Do I pay up to buy the stock and purchase liquidity, or do I wait and hope that liquidity comes to me?" Every trader faces this now-or-later dilemma unless the trade is a run-of-the-mill, easily completed trade. Liquidity is not free. The trader either pays for it implicitly in time (i.e., by incurring delay costs) or pays for it explicitly by paying a higher price in the marketplace to complete the trade with greater immediacy. When should the trader pay for liquidity? How is he or she to determine how much the liquidity is worth? Finally, how can best execution be defined so that it recognizes this critical trade-off?

In this presentation, I will approach this trade-off between cost and liquidity as part of a larger discussion of the AIMR Trade Management Guidelines (TMG).[1] As a member of the task force that created the guidelines, I will highlight some of the key issues we grappled with as we worked out these guidelines.

What Is Best Execution?

In 1993, Wagner and Edwards defined best execution as "the process most likely to flow the maximum investment decision value into the portfolios."[2] The AIMR TMG echos this statement: Best execution is "the trading process Firms apply that seeks to maximize the value of a client's portfolio within the client's stated investment objectives and constraints" (p. 4). Notice that both of these definitions focus on the value-to-cost equation—the balance between the total cost the client ultimately pays and the value the client receives in exchange. This view is broader than simply focusing on securing the lowest cost trade. It clearly recognizes the now-or-later nature of the cost versus liquidity trade-off.

The U.S. SEC has said that best execution is "a duty to seek the most favorable execution terms reasonably available given the specific circumstances of each trade."[3] These circumstances include the size of the order, trading characteristics, availability of information on market centers, cost, and difficulty. Unlike the AIMR definition, the SEC definition says nothing about the value of completing the trade, which I find a little shortsighted. If I were asked to rewrite the definition I would add three points:

- the reason for the trade—the information content and urgency of the trade, which are known primarily to the portfolio manager,
- the specific goals and objectives the manager has for the trade—for example, how quickly the portfolio manager needs to have the trade done, and
- the expected value that will accrue to the portfolio as a result of the judicious purchase of liquidity, if needed.

---

[1] The AIMR TMG can be accessed at www.aimr.org/pdf/standards/trademgmt_guidelines.pdf.
[2] Wayne H. Wagner and Mark Edwards, "Best Execution," *Financial Analysts Journal* (January/February 1993):65–71.
[3] "Disclosure of Order Execution and Routing Practices," SEC Final Rule No. 34-43590 (27 November 2000). This ruling can be accessed at www.sec.gov/rules/final/34-43590.htm.

In other words, I would define best execution within the framework of what the client ultimately pays and what the client receives in exchange.

The U.S. Department of Labor (DOL) in administering ERISA has issued DOL Technical Release 86-1, which says that advisors should "periodically and systematically" evaluate the quality of the services that the advisor and its clients are getting from the brokers with whom the advisor places client trades.[4] Although the phrase "periodically and systematically" *implies* an analysis of the costs of trading and *the benefits received from the brokers,* it is not explicitly stated. Thus, from a regulatory standpoint, both the SEC and DOL definitions are silent on the value of the trade to the client's portfolio, which is a big shortcoming relative to the AIMR TMG definition.

In contrast, AIMR (in the TMG) has defined best execution correctly; AIMR put the definition of best execution in the context of what the client ultimately pays and the investment value the client receives in exchange. As articulated in the TMG, the AIMR definition recognizes that best execution

- is intrinsically tied to the portfolio-decision value and cannot be evaluated independently,
- is a prospective, statistical, and qualitative concept that cannot be known with certainty *ex ante*,
- has aspects that may be measured and analyzed over time on an *ex post* basis, even though accurate measurement on a trade-by-trade basis may not be meaningful in isolation, and
- is interwoven into complicated, repetitive, and continuing practices and relationships. (p. 4)

The first point acknowledges the need to consider not only the cost of the trade but also the investment value of the security purchased at that cost. The second point states that best execution is prospective (i.e., looks into the future). Thus, best execution begins before the trade starts. Trading is a *process*, and best execution is the *standard* by which this process is judged. The second point also states that best execution "cannot be known with certainty" before the fact. In other words, traders have to decide what represents best execution before they begin to trade. Then, of course, they must adapt to the information that they receive from the marketplace.

As to the third point, I personally believe that accurate measurement on a trade-by-trade basis is feasible and not that complicated to do. In my view, however, the really meaningful measure of an individual trade is rarely statistically significant. Why? Because participants in the marketplace are constantly arriving, interacting, and departing. As a result, price is unstable. It is difficult to determine whether or not best execution was achieved on an individual trade. Indeed, the TMG standard explicitly does not require a trade-by-trade evaluation. For an accurate measurement, a statistical concept needs to be applied to aggregate the data and dampen the variability inherent in individual, noisy trade observations. The fourth point claims that best execution relies on "continuing practices and relationships," which depend on trust and fidelity. We certainly have fidelity and trust from anonymous and secure electronic communications networks (ECNs). Trust is not an issue on an electronic platform because the trader controls the information given to the ECN and thus it cannot be leaked to the broader market. But whenever human beings enter the trading process as intermediaries, trust or fidelity must be continuously monitored and earned.

AIMR Implementation Recommendations

AIMR's TMG defines best execution accurately by stating the concept in terms of the costs and the value received in exchange for the costs. But then a disconnect arises between the definition of best execution and the guidelines that address the procedures and documentation for assuring and supporting best execution within a firm.

The procedures and documentation that AIMR recommends start with establishing an oversight review committee. Representatives to that committee should be drawn from all the areas in a firm that are affected by best execution, including portfolio management and security analysis. Then, the recommendations suggest collecting and studying relevant trade and service data so that trading evaluations can be made, and they advise that the data be reviewed at least quarterly. The next step is collecting and maintaining a file of key findings and decisions about the process, and the final step is documenting these findings and being prepared to disclose them, especially when SEC examiners ask the firm to demonstrate that it is achieving best execution.

Notice, however, that these recommendations do not address the concept of portfolio value. In my opinion, a last and final recommendation should be to act on the findings in order to improve the process. Unless a firm can draw insights from this analysis that it can use to improve trading in the future, the recommendations as they stand now do not amount to much.

---

[4] Securities Exchange Act Release No. 34-23170, 17 C.F.R. 241.23170 (23 April 1986). More information about this release can be accessed at www.securities.state.oh.us/Bulletin/BUL012.pdf.

So, with all due respect, I do not think that creating documents to reside in the file cabinet will help the trading process. These recommendations are only worth following if they lead to changed perceptions and assumptions on the part of the manager and the trader. After all, these are the two people who are initiating and controlling the trading process. If I asked a portfolio manager and a trader how they could improve best execution, they would probably say that they are already operating at the highest efficiency. Indeed, within their frame of reference I would agree with them. Thus, the AIMR recommendations will only generate new insights if managers and traders are encouraged to widen their points of view. For example, if a trader's position is that his goal is to get the best price for the trades he is trying to execute, he may push the objective of securing the value of the trade into the background, believing that the value is the portfolio manager's problem. It is not. Value capture is intrinsic to the *raison d'être* of the trading function. Remember, the process revolves around balancing value and cost.

Trade Data

We at the Plexus Group recently conducted a study of the aggregated order and trading data from all of our clients, which resulted in our being able to analyze nearly three-quarters of a million portfolio manager orders.[5] We sorted these trades based on market value, from the smallest trade to the largest trade, and then divided the trades into five groups (quintiles) so that each group represented the same number of dollars traded.

In the first quintile were the smallest orders, encompassing only 20 percent of the dollars traded but 92.5 percent of the orders represented. These trades averaged 2,000 shares, $50,000 in principal, and less than one-half of a percent of a day's trading volume in the stock. On average, the cost was 6 bps, excluding commissions.

At the other end of the spectrum, the fifth quintile, were the largest trades. For this 20 percent of the dollars traded, the trades averaged 2.1 million shares, $81 million in principal, and 56 percent of the daily volume in the stock. Their average cost was 127 bps, excluding commissions.

First-quintile trades are routine trades. For these trades, the SEC, DOL, and AIMR procedures make sense, but we believe that these trades are not the ones that will make a difference in a portfolio's value. Rather, it is the fifth-quintile trades that make a difference—those in which the portfolio manager bets a significant portion of his or her future performance on establishing a major position or removing one from the portfolio. It is very difficult to make a major impact on portfolio value with smaller trades, other than perhaps cutting commission costs and executing as quickly as possible so that the important trades, the ones representing the major bets made by the manager, receive the warranted attention.

Certainly, there is no excuse for paying more than necessary, but sometimes, particularly on fifth-quintile trades, investment considerations dominate so that the best trading process is the one most likely to maximize the value of the client's portfolio. I cannot emphasize often enough that effective trading is not about cost; it is about managing the cost/benefit ratio. Best execution means capturing the net value of a trade; it does not necessarily mean reducing the cost. A trade that is large and laden with timely information may require that the trader buy liquidity to complete the manager's strategy in a timely manner. If the trader does not purchase the liquidity, that trade is subject to delay costs, which represent, in our computations, the largest portion of overall transaction costs. Costs are important, but they are secondary to the value of the investment strategy.

Perspectives

As a member of the task force that put together the AIMR TMG, I have an inside view on the process and the outcome of the TMG, from which I wish to share five key perspectives.

Perspective #1. The purpose of trading is to capture the value of investment decisions. Thus, any definition of best execution is part and parcel of the definition of *prudent expert* that guides fiduciary decisions. Consequently, a definition of best execution existed prior to the AIMR guidelines; it was just not articulated. The DOL charges an investment manager with a duty to act as a prudent expert with respect to the management of fiduciary decisions. The portfolio manager is clearly a prudent expert, but the portfolio manager's security selection and portfolio construction processes count for naught until the transactions are completed. Therefore, the trader is also a prudent expert and is accountable to fiduciary standards.

Perspective #2. Best execution is not an outcome; it is a process. It applies to the way traders (and managers) conduct themselves as they are trading. The standards are before-the-fact behavioral, not after-the-fact consequential. To be effective, the standards must be known, in place, and executed with

---

[5] For more information on this study, see Wayne Wagner's preconference workshop presentation "Institutional Order Flow and the Hurdles to Superior Performance" in this proceedings.

fidelity before the fact. In other words, the definition is for a process that, practically speaking, is unique to each investment management shop. The specific results—the unique executions—intermingle with unforeseeable and uncontrollable variables throughout the execution process. An unexpectedly expensive trade result does not make the process wrong; it actually makes it right.

Perspective #3. The common wisdom is that on every trade there is a winner and a loser. If the buyer won, then the seller lost, and vice versa. Suppose the buyer was able to buy at a discount. Did the seller then have a bad execution? Not necessarily. The seller may have had a good reason to complete the trade quickly—to purchase liquidity immediately rather than waiting on the hope of a subsequently better price.

Every trade is different; therefore, best execution is situational and contextual. The point is that best execution has to be defined so that both buyer and seller can achieve it on the same trade. Trading involves two processes, buying and selling, conducted simultaneously, and both of them may easily meet the definition of actions carried out by a prudent expert. This is a win–win, not a zero-sum, game.

Perspective #4. Trading occurs in a high-variability environment. Every trade tells something, but not everything, about the quality of the process. Think of a bridge player. A bridge player cannot be evaluated fairly on how well or poorly an individual hand was played. The evaluator needs to observe how the player adapted to the variety of situations that arose in playing the entire game.

In the constantly evolving and changing world of the trader, defining a good trade and a bad trade is not possible. Although nearly all traders will say that they can tell a good trade from a bad trade, they cannot substantiate the claim. Because of this high level of uncertainty, trade evaluation must rely on statistical analysis. Data from multiple trades must be aggregated to allow meaningful conclusions to be made about trading value.

Perspective #5. Despite the variability and uncertainty inherent in the conduct of an individual trade, aggregated trade data contain information useful in evaluating the process. Each period generates further, more timely information.

I believe that the trading-evaluation process should consist of eight steps. The first four steps pertain to an individual trade:
1. Execute the order (the action that the following process will evaluate).
2. Record the information associated with the trade.
3. Capture that information.
4. Measure execution costs.

In recording the information about the trade, the evaluator needs to know not only the details of the trade, such as number of shares and price, but also when the portfolio manager gave the order to the trader, when the trader sent the order to the broker, and what, if any, parameters (such as limits or urgency indications) the manager gave the trader and/or the trader gave the broker.

The second four steps examine the information gathered by the first four steps for the purpose of improving the trading process so as to enhance the process in the future:
5. Benchmark the trade against an objective standard that adjusts for the difficulty of the trade.
6. Aggregate the data by sector, country, buy versus sell trades—any combination that might provide useful insights.
7. Identify the lower quality trading situations and devise means of potential improvement.
8. Implement any changes suggested by the analyses. The sole reason to analyze the data is to ask: "What can we do better in the future?" This step is the crux of the whole process. It is the essence of best execution—a never ending quest for ways to improve portfolio performance.

The evidence says that these steps are effective. Plexus recently studied the trading for every new client that had been with us for two years. We compared the clients' trading costs in the first quarter they came to Plexus with their costs one and two years later. We documented an average savings of 38 percent. The savings were not generated across the board but occurred in specific situations. Once these situations were identified, it was possible to make improvements and further the cause of future "best execution" practices. By measuring and analyzing all execution costs, including liquidity, a firm can prove that the portfolio manager adds value to the client's portfolio through his or her decision-making process and that the value of the trade was worth the cost of the trade.

Figure 1 is a graphical illustration of these eight steps and divides the process into three parts. First, a firm has to record and measure not only the details of the orders that it executed but also the market environment in which those orders were executed. Second, the firm has to aggregate the data it has recorded in a way that makes sense for the firm and compare that data with appropriate benchmarks, such as a cost benchmark or a peer-group universe. Third, the firm must evaluate each individual contribution to the quality of the trading process in all relevant contexts. For example:

Figure 1. A "Best Practices" Approach

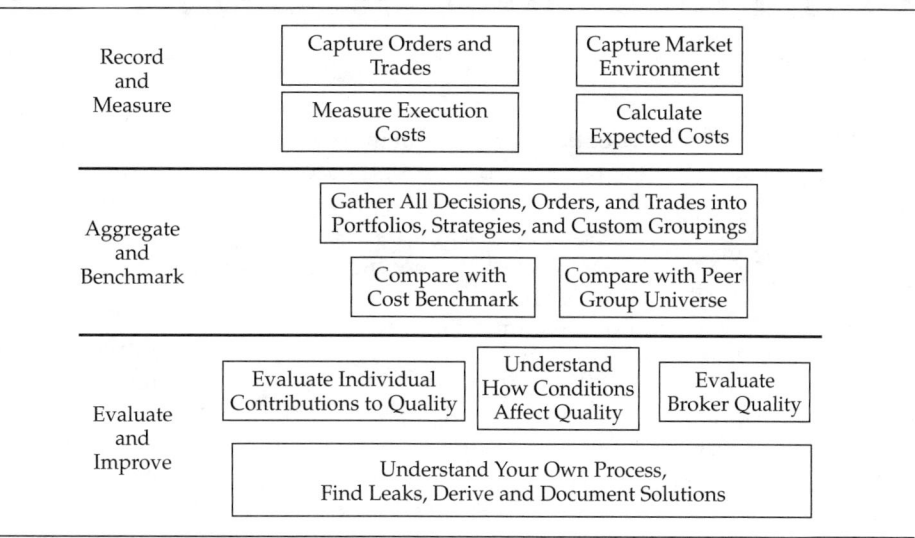

Record and Measure	Capture Orders and Trades	Capture Market Environment
	Measure Execution Costs	Calculate Expected Costs
Aggregate and Benchmark	Gather All Decisions, Orders, and Trades into Portfolios, Strategies, and Custom Groupings	
	Compare with Cost Benchmark	Compare with Peer Group Universe
Evaluate and Improve	Evaluate Individual Contributions to Quality	Understand How Conditions Affect Quality	Evaluate Broker Quality
	Understand Your Own Process, Find Leaks, Derive and Document Solutions		

- What did each broker add to the process?
- How do the conditions under which trades are executed affect the quality of the trading?
- What is the quality of trades that have directions attached by the portfolio manager?
- What is the quality of directed commission trades, and is it the same for trades that are not so encumbered?

Conclusion

The bottom line is that a firm must understand its own trading process and find any leaks that may be reducing trading efficiency and hampering best execution. These leaks are not found across the board but are in specific places. Once the leaks are found, a firm should fix the biggest ones first. Over time, execution will slowly improve. The AIMR TMG counsels a firm to derive and document solutions, but in my opinion, a firm does not need another report to put in the file cabinet. A firm needs a solution to its trading problems that can only be found in a thorough analysis of the data. In that sense, the AIMR guidelines stop one step too soon.

Ultimately, everyone who touches the trade has an obligation to provide best execution: The exchange, broker, trader, portfolio manager, and plan sponsor—all play a role in best execution. A good way to think about best execution is as the interlocking links of a chain; each person (link) must work with all the others to form a strong, viable trading process (chain).

> # Question and Answer Session
Wayne H. Wagner

Question: Would the unbundling of services help better define best execution?

Wagner: Yes. We are simply going to have to learn to deal in a world where a function such as research is paid for separately. It will be a much cleaner world.

A trader's job 10–15 years ago was primarily to keep track of the firm's soft-dollar obligations. Execution wasn't the primary focus at all. Instead, the focus was "How much do I have to pay this broker? How much do I have to pay that broker? How do I keep track of it?"

That tracking is still a large, and in my view a largely fruitless, part of the job of trying to get performance into portfolios. The industry has traditionally thought of the commission as free money, and it has distorted our thinking about the trading process.

My general belief is that the broker should be expected to earn the right to get the trade every time, on every single trade. You are not going to get best execution on any trade that is precommitted to a broker. We've seen it with directed commissions, and we've definitely seen it with wrap fees.

Bundling is going to change once people get worried about their firm's next U.S. SEC examination. Trading based on wrap accounts and other relationships will have to be justified to the SEC.

Question: How do soft-dollar arrangements fit into your process?

Wagner: With soft-dollar trades, you have to rely on your relationships with your brokers. You're very important to them, and you have to lean on that relationship to ensure you get the best execution on soft-dollar trades.

Question: Would an investment manager forgo potentially profitable investments that might be in the client's interest if we moved toward a world where firms were forced to unbundle services and absorb commission fees?

Wagner: The question is whether we are generating trades simply because they appear to be free and they bring with them services that might not appear to be so valuable if we put our own money into buying those services. Under the existing system, the management firm and the manager are motivated to get good performance. If a manager thinks she has a valuable idea, she's going to fight for it, and she's going to fight for the budget to be able to carry out that idea.

Let's assume that this cadre of analysts at the big brokerage firms can't be paid with a soft-dollar budget. Research could be paid for in cash that would come from an increase in fees, or these analysts could be used exclusively by their own firms in their investment management divisions. If the research is valuable, it might give the firm a competitive advantage because the firm would have exclusive access to that research. Or other firms might end up hiring these research analysts and using them exclusively at their firms. Doing away with soft dollars would be a momentous change in this industry.

Question: Where do step-outs, which allow a firm to allocate part of a trade to another broker, fit in the trading process?

Wagner: Step-outs raise an important question: What is the knowledge of trading interest worth to the broker? We are now *giving* that information to the brokerage industry. We try to hide it from them, but we're not totally successful. Why shouldn't we *sell* that information to them? Knowing where the trading interest lies represents an advantage to a brokerage.

Question: The Perold implementation shortfall methodology presupposes that you can measure the slippage between a portfolio manager's idea and the trade report. Can most buy-side firms capture the price at idea time?

Wagner: The portfolio manager might have had the idea in the shower that morning, and that kind of information cannot be recorded. But I think that's irrelevant. An idea is only actionable when the portfolio manager opens his or her mouth and says "I want to buy" or "I want to sell." Anything before that point doesn't affect the trading process at all.

Nevertheless, we start from the moment a trade occurs and then look back 10 days to determine whether this portfolio manager was the first to buy or the last to buy on a piece of news. We are trying to determine the responsiveness of the manager to news. You're not a very good portfolio manager if you wait until everything is proved because the news is already embedded in the price.

Question: You spoke of capturing the urgency of a trading decision. How do portfolio managers know how urgent a trade is without knowing the ultimate outcome?

Wagner: Who says the urgency of a trade can't be updated? If a change in status is recorded, it can be analyzed. You can analyze where the manager changed (or didn't change) the trade's urgency relative to the characteristics of the trade.

What is important is that a firm has a dynamic process in place that changes moment by moment with the conduct of the trade. The discipline of having a manager identify which trades are the important ones is a good strategy.

Ten years ago, we asked our clients how they prioritized trades, and "alphabetically" was the most frequent answer. I think we've come a long way.

Question: Why do firms continue to use volume-weighted average price (VWAP) for trade cost analysis rather than, for example, implementation shortfall?

Wagner: For the 92 percent of trading activity that averages 2,000 shares, I don't have any problem with using VWAP. At the other extreme, if your trading activity in a stock is 100 percent of the stock's daily volume, it doesn't matter what price you paid; you'll still meet the VWAP, so you have to be very careful and judicious in the use of VWAP to make sure it is giving you valuable information. Every speaker today has said that the implementation shortfall approach, although it is certainly more difficult to put in place and to understand than VWAP, is the source of the information that will allow you to deliver better execution and performance.

Question: How does the U.S. market compare in trade quality with other markets around the world?

Wagner: We at the Plexus Group looked at 68 different countries in a side-by-side comparison on trade quality using an implementation shortfall approach. We tried to adjust for the thinness of some of the stocks and the fact that you don't get many trades in Lithuania, for example. And guess what? We may complain about our markets in the United States, but they're as good as we can measure anywhere in the world. Some others, such as the United Kingdom, come close.

The market system that we have in the United States is very good, although it is not good enough in my mind. It looks to me like we have an institutional market imposed on a retail structure. That's great for the retail market, but it isn't so good for the institutional market. We need a market where size can meet size and a fair exchange can be negotiated. Liquidnet and Harborside are trying to do that.

Question: Could you recommend some good references for more information?

Wagner: Read Larry Harris's book *Trading and Exchanges: Market Microstructure for Practitioners*.[1] A series of helpful commentaries can be found at www.plexusgroup.com.

---

[1] Larry Harris, *Trading and Exchanges: Market Microstructure for Practitioners* (Oxford, U.K.: Oxford University Press, 2002).

The Impact of the Myners Report on Global Investors

Marcus Hooper
Managing Director
Duvacy Ltd.
London

> The British government commissioned a review of trading costs and procedural distortions in the institutional investment process, especially as they affect pension fund returns. The resulting study, commonly known as the "Myners Report," suggests more disclosure from institutional money managers, which has led to an increased focus on transaction costs.

On 6 March 2001, Paul Myners released a report entitled "Institutional Investment in the United Kingdom: A Review" (henceforth known as the "Myners Report").[1] Myners, a graduate of the University of London and current chairman of Wellington Reinsurance, had been asked by the U.K. Treasury to investigate distortions in institutional investment decision making. In particular, the Treasury was interested in whether certain barriers were preventing institutional investors from investing in private equity. As part of his investigation, Myners found that "an important cost to pension funds, namely brokerage commission, is subject to insufficient scrutiny. Clearer and more rigorous disciplines could be applied to these costs, which are substantial" (p. 2). Although the issue of commissions is a small part of the report, the press seized on this issue and it has become a major driver of change in the United Kingdom.

In this presentation, I will discuss the impact that the Myners Report has had on the trading and investment management communities in the United Kingdom as well as the global implications of the report.

Key Issues and Questions

In the aftermath of the Myners Report, some key issues and questions have arisen.

How Is the Myners Report Changing Industry Behavior in Europe? One significant change resulting from the Myners Report is an increased interest in trading costs, which is an extremely good outcome. Also, the consultants to plan sponsors are becoming more involved in transaction cost analysis and are now selling more services in this field. Furthermore, consultancy in this area is now exceedingly popular, in contrast to the past.

As a result of the report's findings, pension fund trustees are having to learn about trading costs. They must understand these costs because these costs affect the value of the pension fund's portfolio.

Finally, the industry has responded by introducing new disclosure recommendations.

What Are the New Disclosure Recommendations? The Myners Report is a comment on good practice rather than a suggestion of specific rules. The industry is getting closer to specific rules, but it is not there yet. The industry is still trying to understand the implications of the new disclosure recommendations, and believe me, they are more significant and far reaching than is generally understood.

One direct result of the Myners Report was that two industry groups—the Investment Management Association (IMA) and the National Association of Pension Funds (NAPF)—formulated a joint *voluntary* code of practice.[2] Firms can subscribe to it or not as they choose, but in fact, most pension fund managers have indeed subscribed to it.

Editor's note: Marcus Hooper's presentation reflects his own personal comments, opinions, and ideas and not those of any firm.

[1] This report can be accessed at www.hm-treasury.gov.uk/Documents/Financial_Services/Securities_and_Investments/fin_sec_mynfinal.cfm.

[2] "The Investment Management Association Pension Fund Disclosure Code" can be accessed at www.investmentuk.org/investmentuk/about_ima/reports/pfdcode.pdf.

The code has two levels. Level One covers the policies, processes, and procedures that investment managers should follow; Level Two is more specific and asks managers to supply various details and specific numbers. In my opinion, some dislocation exists between the two levels of the code.

What Is the Impact on Transparency and Accountability? In the past, transparency in trading costs and trade management was all but nonexistent, and no real accountability for these costs existed either. Unfortunately, not much has changed and there remains only minimal transparency for the end customer. But the issue of accountability for trading costs is driving change in the industry. Who should be accountable for trading costs within asset management firms? That is a question that must be addressed.

If the industry were to provide information beyond the IMA/NAPF disclosure recommendations, would it be of any use? If managers supplied this information, could customers interpret it, use it, and benefit from it? The industry needs to be heavily involved in educating the end customer as to what the recommendations are and what they mean, but a separate question is whether the customer needs to understand the specific details.

The Myners Report raises the possibility of unbundling trading services. The underlying issue of unbundling has a great deal more to do with transparency and accountability than with market structure. Unbundled commissions have direct and significant implications for soft dollars and commission recapture practices.

What Are the Global Effects of U.K. Change? The Myners Report has had a big impact on investors in the United Kingdom, and likewise, investors around the world are thinking carefully about the issues of transaction costs. Certainly, the interest in transaction costs and transaction cost analysis in the United Kingdom mirrors research taking place in the United States.

The approach taken by the Myners Report is quite specific and quite unique. Thus, I find it difficult to imagine that the whole world, or even the rest of Europe, would move to the U.K. model. A great deal of structural change has to happen before that transformation can occur.

Where Are We Today? More than two years have passed since the Myners Report was published. Does the industry now have its act together? Has the industry solved the issue of transaction cost analysis? What are the subsequent issues that must be addressed? And who decides the next step, if there is a next step? I am not sure that these issues have been completely addressed in the United Kingdom.

Recap of Events

Before going into more detail, I would like to give a quick recap of the events related to the Myners Report.

Early March 2001—Myners Report Published. The Myners Report was released on 6 March 2001. In the report, Myners suggested that asset managers themselves pay hard dollars explicitly for research services:

> The review recommends that it is good practice for institutional investment management mandates to incorporate a management fee inclusive of any external research, information or transaction services acquired or used by the fund manager, rather than these costs being passed on to the client. (p. 22)

Although only 2 out of the 201 pages in the report address commission payments, commission payments have been the main focus of attention.

Early October 2001—Myners' 10 Questions Published. When the Myners Report was published, it created a flurry in the press and sparked some criticism within the industry. Myners realized that the situation was getting a little bit out of control. To defend his recommendations, he published "Transaction Costs: Questions for Fund Managers" (published 2 October 2001).[3] This list of 10 questions raised two concerns: Controlling transaction costs is easier said than done, and the addition of market impact and opportunity costs to the total transaction cost bill is likely to increase the work and expense involved in managing securities portfolios.

2002—IMA/NAPF Joint Voluntary Code. The IMA/NAPF joint voluntary code was issued in 2002. It is a joint effort between asset managers and plan sponsors to address the issues surrounding commission payments that are raised in the Myners Report.

Effect of the Report

The Myners Report has affected the industry in numerous ways, ranging from an increase in the use of transaction cost analysis to a more proactive stance by the industry in addressing transaction cost issues.

Transaction Cost Analysis Is Hot. Transaction cost analysis is astoundingly popular at the moment. It is *the* hot topic. But the problem is that hardly anyone in the United Kingdom really understands it! This general lack of understanding is the result of transaction cost analysis having been associated solely with the trading function rather than with the

---

[3]This document can be accessed at www.hm-treasury.gov.uk/documents/financial_services/securities_and_investments/fin_sec_mynquests.cfm.

entire business—the investment management process. Education and objective research are definitely needed in this area. Most of the information in the public domain is biased because it is produced by industry participants or vendors.

Consultants Are Delighted. Consultants are absolutely delighted about the heightened interest in transaction cost analysis. They have been trying for years to sell better ways of picking fund managers, and this gem of a marketing opportunity has been thrown into their laps. Investors can now select asset managers based on transaction costs, an entirely new aspect. I firmly believe that the majority of the performance difference between the top quartile and the bottom quartile of fund managers involves trading costs, so being able to select managers based on information about their transaction cost management skills can have a big impact on overall performance.

The problem is that the consultants do not understand all the issues surrounding transaction cost analysis any more than investors do. In fact, they have very little knowledge of the subject at all. I am not being unfair when I make this statement. Up to now, they simply have not covered this subject and, therefore, are not positioned to do this kind of work. But all of a sudden, transaction cost management issues have been foisted on them. Getting up to speed on the issues is no small task, especially when the industry itself is not well positioned to support the education effort.

One development that really scares me is that pension fund trustees have suddenly awakened to the transaction cost issue and have reacted in a dangerous way. They have told their asset managers to benchmark their performance against particular indexes, often because the vendors of transaction cost analysis products have recommended the benchmarks. Although such a move is the trustees' prerogative, the danger is that these benchmarks may have inherent biases that are counterproductive to good investment management.

ATS Are Delighted. Alternative trading systems (ATS) think the Myners Report is wonderful because transaction cost analysis often shows that crossing networks are cheaper than conventional methods of trading.[4] The problem is that different orders require different trading methods, so explicit trading cost should not drive the trading decision. Rather, opportunity costs should also be considered.

I am as big a supporter of crossing networks as anyone. They serve a very useful purpose, but they are not right for every single trade. I love the idea of a single, central call auction, which the crossing net-

---
[4] See Jennifer Conrad's presentation in this proceedings.

works could provide; but they do not at the moment. Unless the U.K. government requires that all trades go to a crossing network, those investors who submit trades to a crossing network may suffer opportunity costs from the potential lack of liquidity. I am not saying crossing networks have no place; they do. They just should not be used exclusively in any given situation.

Influence on Buy-Side Trader Thinking Is Lacking. Not much has changed in buy-side trader thinking since the Myners Report was published. I know the buy-side trading community in London rather well, and most traders still do not recognize the importance of transaction cost analysis. The average buy-side trader only wants to buy and sell stocks in the biggest size possible all day long, not work out whether he or she did a good job at it. The trader thinks to himself or herself, "Of course I did a good job. I am a good trader." The problem is that often the transaction cost analysis says otherwise. Many buy-side traders are devising how to game benchmarks, so while the trader may be beating the benchmark, he or she may also be actively destroying portfolio value.

Buy-side traders may lose out entirely if they do not respond to the challenges they are now facing. The question has been raised as to whether traders should be considered prudent experts. I do not think that members of the U.K. buy-side community are prudent experts. I do not see how they possibly can be because they are not given entire freedom to trade where and how they need to.

Keep in mind, however, that as far as trading goes, a difference exists between the United Kingdom and the rest of Europe. U.K. buy-side trading has been embedded in the overall investment management process for a long time. In contrast, only recently have investment managers in continental Europe created specialized functions or teams for trading. A lot of continental European trading desks are being formed now—facing, head-on, issues such as those raised in the Myners Report. They are at an advantage because they do not have to incorporate new ideas into an already established trading desk. They are approaching these issues in a fresh state of mind.

Industry Is Now Proactive. As a result of the report, the industry has become active in addressing trading cost issues after many years of ignoring them. An example of this proactive stance is the joint voluntary code created by the IMA and the NAPF.

IMA/NAPF Recommendations

As I explained earlier, the IMA/NAPF code has two levels. Level One covers the policies, processes, and procedures that investment managers should follow;

Level Two is more specific and covers the information that managers should report.

Level One. Level One is fairly straightforward and deals with trading methods and venues. It requires that firms disclose with whom they trade—brokers, ATS, crossing networks, and so on. Firms must also specify how they do their trading—net, commission, program trading, and so on. In addition, firms must state what their selection criteria are for brokers, how they produce their commission targets, and how they decide to split their trades between commission, net business, soft dollars, and so forth. The code also requires that firms specify *how* they measure trading costs, although the code contains no recommendation *to* measure trading costs! Finally, Level One of the code states that firms must explain conflicts of interest and the use of internal versus external research. The focus on internal versus external research is interesting. One firm I know decided roughly four years ago to hire about 25 research analysts to produce internal research. But in late 2002, this firm eliminated all of its research analysts because keeping them was simply not cost-effective. The firm decided that it could get this research expertise more cheaply externally.

Level Two. Whereas Level One instructs firms on what types of information to report, Level Two instructs firms on what detailed numbers they should report. **Exhibit 1** is extracted from the IMA/NAPF recommendations and shows the information that these organizations expect firms to supply. A criticism of these recommendations is that they cater to the lowest common denominator. They were designed to make sure that the smallest firms can produce the requested information.

All the information requested for disclosure under the IMA/NAPF code can be interesting, but I am not convinced of its usefulness to a client. The only value I see it offering a client is in setting up commission recapture programs. And the only explicit information that is being requested by the IMA/NAPF recommendations is on commissions. The recommendations show complete ignorance of underlying market impact and opportunity costs. Perhaps I am just being skeptical, but the possibility exists that a firm can meet the Level One recommendations and not even be able to answer the Level Two recommendations.

Transparency and Accountability

Prior to the Myners Report, most transaction costs lacked transparency. If firms are now following the IMA/NAPF recommendations, then some small progress has been made in this regard. Many firms using transaction cost analysis, however, are not using it properly because they adopted it as a knee-jerk reaction when regulators questioned them about best execution. Their response was to acquire transaction cost analysis tools and throw the results at the regulators as proof that they value and aspire to best execution. These criticisms of poor transparency do not apply to soft-dollar commissions, however, which have strong regulatory controls in the United Kingdom and are actually very transparent.

I must come back again to my earlier question: Does the client genuinely require all the information stipulated in the IMA/NAPF recommendations? The answer partially depends on client sophistication. For a very sophisticated client, the information currently

Exhibit 1. Example Report: Summary of Trading Volumes, Commissions, and Fees

Counterparty	Total	Traded Net	Subject to Commissions	Total	Under Softing Arrangements	Under Directed or Recapture Arrangements	Other
	£000	£000	£000	£000	£000	£000	£000
1							
2							
:							
9							
10							
Others >5%							
:							
Others (total)							
Total							
% age	100%	[ ]%	[ ]%	100%	[ ]%	[ ]%	[ ]%

disclosed is all very well, but for a less sophisticated customer, the information should be offered in plain English, but this type of communication is not happening. The danger is that moderately sophisticated clients may misunderstand the information and its contextual aspects and agree to a bad policy that ultimately damages their portfolios' performance.

Transaction Cost Analysis

A severe lack of education and understanding surrounds transaction cost analysis at all levels. Fund managers do not understand it; consultants do not understand it; trustees certainly do not understand it; and dealers themselves, in general, do not understand it. This problem leads to potential abuse of transaction cost analysis results.

For the most part, asset managers have not driven the changes that have occurred in the industry related to transaction cost analysis. Rather, third parties with a vested interest and the regulators have been heavily involved in influencing the direction of these changes. With the lack of interest and the *laissez faire* attitude the buy side has shown, the investment management industry should be fearful that its reaction (or lack thereof) will be interpreted as evidence that a critical aspect of client performance, best execution, is being ignored. So far, the industry has escaped this criticism; and as yet, no one has filed a class action lawsuit against an asset manager for ignoring this issue.

In the United Kingdom, the full array of trading costs is only now becoming known. Even Myners himself does not refer to the multiple components of transaction costs, although he knows that the total cost, which encompasses all of these components, is significant. His focus is on commissions, which is not the key component. The trading costs that really matter are market impact and opportunity costs. Focusing on total transaction costs increases the work and expense involved in managing securities portfolios, but holding asset managers accountable for these costs is reasonable and fair.

Following is a very simple example of a transaction cost analysis issue that looks at volume-weighted average price (VWAP) or open, high, low, close (OHLC) as a comparative benchmark. Suppose I executed an order over three days. **Figure 1** shows what happened on those three days. If I, or any trader, saw live price information throughout the day, I could generally work out what the VWAP or OHLC would be. It is not that difficult. On Day 1, I bought stock at a price of 139 euros; the VWAP was 140 euros. On Day 2, I bought at a price of 159 euros; the VWAP was 160 euros. On Day 3, I bought at a price of 179 euros; the VWAP was 180 euros. Afterwards, when I evaluated my trading skill using

Figure 1. Transaction Cost Analysis Using VWAP/OHLC

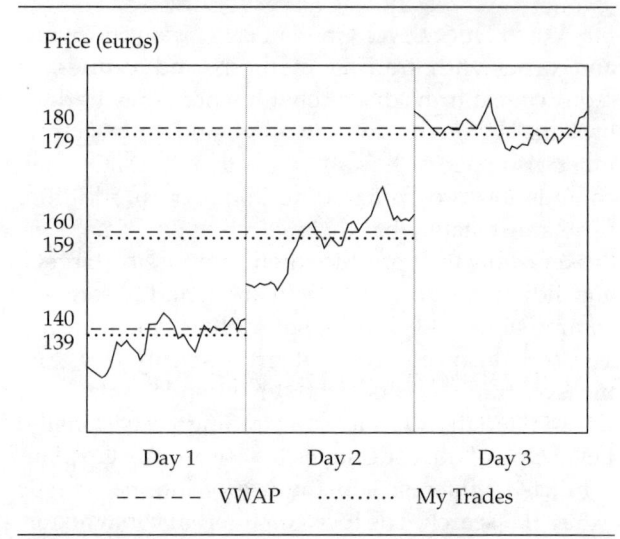

VWAP, I saw that I did very well. On each day, I beat VWAP by 1 euro, which translated into 71 bps on Day 1, 62 bps on Day 2, and 56 bps on Day 3. I bought 100,000 shares each day, and I saved between 56 bps and 71 bps on each share. At 1 euro per share, that was a savings of 300,000 euros. I am a genius. I must be the best trader ever!

Another interpretation, however, exists when my performance benchmark is implementation shortfall. Suppose on Day 1, I was offered all 300,000 shares of the stock at a price of 145 euros, but I turned it down because I knew that the VWAP on Day 1 would be around 140 euros. I made this decision (in retrospect a bad decision) because I knew that my performance as a trader was being measured using the daily VWAP and that if I bought the stock at 145 euros my performance would not look good. But think about what I paid for the stock over the three days. I paid 47.7 million euros for the 300,000 shares of the stock. If I had bought it all at a price of 145 euros, I would have paid only 43.5 million euros. The VWAP benchmark tells me I saved 300,000 euros, but the implementation shortfall benchmark tells me I really spent 4.2 million euros more than I needed to. Although implementation shortfall is not the only way to benchmark trading costs, this example clearly shows the weaknesses of a VWAP benchmark.

Control of the Process

An issue that was not addressed by the Myners Report is who controls the trading process. Keep in mind that trading is not quite the same in U.K. firms as it is in many U.S. firms. In my experience, a U.K. trading desk that exercises significant control over order flow is really quite abnormal, and highly skilled trading staff are rare. Consequently, U.K. buy-side traders typically follow the instructions given to them by fund managers as to with whom they should trade. Counterparty selection is almost entirely driven by the need to reciprocate for research received. Fund managers in the United Kingdom exercise extremely strong control over all aspects of the day-to-day management of their portfolios and, as a consequence, are interested primarily in the stock selection, not the trading costs incurred in implementing the decision. Until this system changes or until fund managers wake up to the realization that lowering transaction costs increases portfolio performance, bad trading decisions will continue to be made.

Commission Disaggregation/ Unbundling

For asset managers, disaggregation/unbundling of trading and research means one of two things: greater accountability (because managers have to prove why they are trading in a particular environment) or reduced profitability (if managers have to pay for research with hard dollars, the cost will reduce the bottom line). The best approach is to increase transparency and accountability to clients, but this idea is not well received by the industry. In the long run, disaggregating research from the trading commission payment is inescapable.

The argument for bundled services is that, from the point of view of the client, bundling must surely give a more effective result because an economy of scale must exist. Ultimately, the end customer will have to pay one way or the other, so why not bundle it all together?

The argument against bundled services is that the cost of generating research does not vary much; it is virtually a fixed cost. Therefore, why should research costs vary based on trading volume (i.e., why should a higher commission be required for the same amount of research simply because more shares are purchased)? The costs are not transparent, and they are not adequately controlled.

The perfect solution would be for clients to select the components of the broker services that they like and do not like. If a client likes Broker A's trading ability and Broker B's research, then the perfect solution is to purchase each separately. It *should* be simple to do, but it is not, and asset managers are trying to reconcile this problem because it is fundamental to resolving the commission unbundling problem. Personally, I do not think it matters who pays for the service at the point of trading because in the final analysis, the cost will always be transferred to the client.

In theory, the model for unbundled services on the sell side should be equally applicable on the buy side. As asset managers, we too are selling bundled services. We have trading desks. We have stock-selection capabilities. The situation is the same, is it not? I think it is possible to unbundle the buy side just as it is possible to unbundle the sell side.

Regulation

The regulators are certainly addressing transaction cost issues, but their efforts may not all be fruitful— although they are generating a great deal of paperwork. In this rather atrocious market, the industry is beginning to view these efforts as unnecessary and is not making an effort equal to that of the regulators in order to progress the issue. Two papers were recently issued by the U.K. Financial Services Authority. One was on ATS, and the other one was on best execution. I participated in a buy-side gathering to advise one of the industry regulatory bodies, and it became apparent to me that I was the only person in the room who had read one of these reports that was being discussed at the meeting, evidence of the lack of effort on the part of many in the industry. The amount of time and effort required to actually address all of the issues the regulators are currently exploring is quite significant. An often-raised question is whether the stock-exchange-based regulatory structure is the correct model; in my opinion, a function-based regulatory structure is more appropriate.

Harmonization of regulations throughout Europe is proving awkward because the European countries have different perspectives on the role of trading in the investment management process. Unless the United Kingdom becomes a recognized and leading voice in regulation in Europe, or a major force in exchange consolidation, its trading model may well not survive.

Myners' Thoughts

To date, Myners is disappointed with the lack of industry change that has followed his report. But he has made an ingenious proposal to combat this lack of interest: Fund managers should have to reveal how the portfolios they manage would have performed if they had not traded their portfolios at all and thus incurred no commission costs, taxes, or other trading costs. He is challenging managers to compare their portfolios on 1 January with what their value would have been on 31 December under a buy-and-hold strategy. Then, managers should compare that hypothetical value with the actual value of their portfolios at 31 December. That exercise would probably be completely shocking to most fund managers because they then have to justify their investment decisions against the alpha hurdle net of transaction costs. Interestingly, the press has picked up on Myners' idea and supports it.

Hot Topics

The Myners Report has called attention to trading issues in Europe, and these issues are now becoming hot topics. The Investment Services Directive (ISD) is being revised to incorporate new views on stronger transparency rules (i.e., mandated pretrade transparency) and concentration rules (i.e., trading through a core exchange).[5]

Best execution is undergoing a major review in the United Kingdom, and a Committee of European Securities Regulators (CESR) policy document on ATS has been issued. The CESR definition of an ATS is a multilateral system—not regulated as a market—that brings together multiple trading interests according to nondiscretionary rules in a way that results in a contract.

How should this definition be applied? All crossing networks are automatically multilateral, but the definition of a crossing network is no longer clear-cut. In the CESR definition, "interests" include indications of interest (bids and offers) as well as real interest (i.e., trades). Thus, the CESR definition may include such systems as simple order-routing networks because they bring together interests, even if the trade is not done there. An ATS does not have to be electronic. Any system that is operating in a nondiscretionary rules-based manner that is not electronic qualifies. So, I would argue that the definition includes almost everything, including manually based brokering operations.

The most contentious U.K. issue is pretrade transparency. Pretrade transparency applies only to price-making systems, not to a "black box" crossing network. But pretrade transparency may also apply to "interests" submitted via electronic communication. Apparently, the rules are not constructed logically; instead, they are designed to capture only certain trades and market participants.

The United Kingdom has taken some bold steps in scrutinizing the costs associated with trading investment securities, but whether the rest of the world will follow the United Kingdom's lead is unclear. Doing so would require the total disaggregation of the research and trading function, which is probably too much to ask at present, but some innovative interim solutions might emerge. If the investment industry in the United Kingdom is forced to unbundle transaction costs and services, a likely scenario is that some sort of cross-subsidization will appear. For example, asset managers with regional overseas offices may realize that they cannot afford to pay for research out of the London office, but they can do so out of the Tokyo office, which could put smaller U.K. asset managers at a competitive disadvantage. Another possibility is that if substantive change occurs in the United Kingdom but not elsewhere, U.K. asset managers may be pushed to trade on overseas markets, where regulation is less stringent.

The U.K. changes have been a long time coming, but change cannot happen overnight. Most of the intellectual and academic arguments for change are wrapped up in the discussion surrounding the Myners Report, and not all countries and markets will agree with the United Kingdom's conclusions. Interestingly, the main pressure in the United Kingdom is coming from the Treasury (more so than the regulators), so any outcome is possible.

Conclusions and Observations

The Myners Report has created a certain amount of panic in the industry—for good reason. Traders, portfolio managers, and pension fund trustees have to learn new tricks very quickly. Consultants are already leaping on the bandwagon, selling transaction cost analysis services. And ATS are also leaping on the bandwagon, misselling transaction cost analysis results—trying to show that trades done on crossing networks look cheap compared with trades done elsewhere. Yet, buy-side trading has hardly changed. The necessary changes—moving control of trading to the buy-side traders and away from the portfolio managers—may actually jeopardize the future of buy-side trading as it is now known simply because of the generally poor quality of buy-side trading at most firms.

The industry's initial reaction to the Myners Report was to produce a response quickly, hence, the IMA/NAPF voluntary code. Unfortunately, the industry, in general, has no understanding of transaction cost analysis, as exemplified by the support of VWAP and OHLC as transaction cost analysis benchmarks. The disaggregation of services and commissions is absolutely necessary, even though it will initially be very painful for the industry. After all, transparency is the key issue in guarding the best interests of the client. Much can be overcome if trading issues and disclosures are explained simply.

The major stumbling block that I see now is what I call the "too-difficult" basket. The industry is examining aspects of the market that are very complex. As a result, falling into the trap of concluding that these areas are too difficult to assess and, therefore, too difficult to change will be easy. No one is denying the level of difficulty, but if every issue is put into the too-difficult basket, then the game is over. Nothing will progress. The industry will stagnate once again. Thus, I see this "too-difficult" attitude as the biggest threat to progress in this area, certainly in the United Kingdom.

---

[5]More information about the ISD and its revision can be found at europa.eu.int/comm/internal_market/en/finances/mobil/isd/.

Question and Answer Session

Marcus Hooper

Question: Why are U.K. managers so oblivious to the impact of transaction costs on the alpha-generation process?

Hooper: Let me give you one political reason. Most chief investment officers are former fund managers. They are not former dealers. They spent their careers focusing on stock selection, not on trading at the best price. So, they do not have much background in transaction cost analysis or much appreciation of how large these costs really are.

Question: How serious are you about the unbundling of the buy side?

Hooper: I am very serious about it, and I think it can be done. If I were a sell-side firm at the moment and I thought my margins were being grossly eroded and that the future was looking pretty rocky for me, one of the things I would want to do is compress my costs. And if I could find ways of isolating and identifying what my true costs were of carrying research, carrying trading, carrying whatever it may be, managing my business would be easier.

If you compress the sell side that hard, what is to stop them from going to the end customer (such as the plan sponsors) and saying, "You have great fund managers. They pick all the right stocks, but they have lousy trading." What is to stop them from going directly to the end clients and cutting you (the asset manager) out of the equation on trading?

Question: If managers paid the costs of trading, what would be the impact on firms of various sizes with vastly different economies of scale?

Hooper: Small firms would struggle to pay the costs of trading in this scenario. But the reality is that there are no economies of scale in trading, so the trading costs that are being borne by the industry are just increasing and increasing.

Question: If managers had to pay their own commissions, resulting in more net business, would the market change from an order-driven market to a quote-driven market and potentially have wider spreads?

Hooper: The London Stock Exchange (LSE) is currently looking at reintroducing stocks on a quote-driven basis. The LSE had phased out its quote-driven system in favor of one that was order driven, but they are thinking about reversing that decision. The order-driven market doesn't serve small-cap stocks well because it doesn't provide enough liquidity. So, going back to a quote-driven market is already starting to happen.

Question: You made the point that ATS and ECNs are "islands" of best execution. What do we do to align and leverage these tools within a persistent process?

Hooper: No one seems to know how to do it, but if anyone can align trading methods in a clean and convenient way, they're going to earn a lot of money.

Question: How will the U.K. regulatory reforms following the Myners Report affect U.S. managers who have U.K. operations?

Hooper: I don't honestly know, and I don't think the U.K. industry knows either. Certainly, there is a potential loophole as I described earlier. A firm that has offices in New York, London, and Tokyo may simply subvert the rules by trading consistently zero commission in London and paying those commissions out of another office.

Whether a U.S. firm will be obligated to abide by these standards, I'm not entirely sure. There might be clarification coming on that point from the regulators fairly soon.

Question: What role will transaction cost analysis play in the process of revision of the ISD and the definition of a European best execution regime?

Hooper: The best I can say is that the alignment of the U.K. and continental European interests is not working out very favorably at the moment. At present, there is no common agreement in Europe as to what best execution is. I think that most European regulators appreciate the importance of transaction cost analysis, but because of the complexity of the subject, each group has a significantly different view from the other.

Market Microstructure and the Regulation of Markets

Lawrence E. Harris
*Chief Economist and Director of the Office of Economic Analysis
U.S. Securities and Exchange Commission
Washington, DC*

> The current market structure is rife with inefficiencies, resulting particularly from market access fees, liquidity rebates, market data revenue, and the use of volume-weighted average price as a trading benchmark. These inefficiencies negatively affect price transparency, best execution, and market competition, but ways may exist to improve market efficiency without resorting to changes in regulation.

I will devote most of my presentation to market inefficiencies created by market access fees and the liquidity rebates that accompany them, offering several possible solutions to the problems they create. I will then present my insights into the issue of market data revenue, once again identifying problems and offering solutions. Finally, I will conclude with a brief discussion of the issues surrounding volume-weighted average price (VWAP).

Before I begin, however, I would like to point out that the U.S. SEC, as a matter of policy, disclaims responsibility for any private publication or statement by any of its employees. The views expressed in this presentation are my own and do not necessarily reflect the views of the Commission or my colleagues on the staff of the Commission.

Access Fees

Since the National Association of Securities Dealers' Alternate Display Facility (ADF) began operating, locked markets and crossed markets have become common. They occur most frequently in very actively traded Nasdaq stocks. Consider a typical locked-market situation. An order to sell a stock at $20 is standing in Nasdaq's SuperMontage, and a bid arrives in Instinet at $20. One would assume that a trade would take place, but none does. Instead, Instinet displays the bid in the ADF. It shows $20 bid/$20 offered; with no spread, the market is locked.

This situation occurs frequently because of access fees. For example, suppose a trader has a standing limit order of $20 on a Nasdaq stock displayed in the ADF. When another trader submits a market order of $20, that second trader must pay the exchange 3 mils (three-tenths of a cent) per share as an access fee. Furthermore, the first trader gets a liquidity rebate of 2 mils per share when the trade is executed, giving the exchange a profit of 1 mil (3 mils − 2 mils) per share. Although the bid–offer spread is quoted at 20/20, the real bid–offer spread is half a penny, that is, the 3 mils to reach the order plus the 2 mils rebated on execution. Because the displayed spread is not the true spread, a transparency problem exists because customers are not seeing the actual price they will pay. If this problem were the only consequence of access fee/liquidity rebate pricing, traders could adapt by simply adding half a penny to the price quoted, but it is far from the only problem.

Competitive Problems. For retail traders, the idea of best execution is simple. They want to get the price that is available in the market. For the dealer, however, best execution means offering the best price. But as I have just demonstrated, the best price includes a spread that is half a penny wider than the spread the dealer can collect, so dealers are effectively being forced out of business.

Typically, I do not defend or promote dealers. I do not believe that the market should be structured to increase dealer profits. It should be structured for the investors and financiers who use the markets, and dealers should be supported only to the extent that they provide service to those for whom the markets ultimately exist. Furthermore, I am not opposed to narrow spreads. But the current application of access fees represents a clear case of dealers being discriminated against by the nature of the system. When the spread, as presented, does not reflect reality and when it hurts the traders who offer liquidity, then a serious problem exists.

Besides creating a lack of transparency and making it impossible for dealers to apply best execution standards as intended, the system also denies buyers and sellers the ability to negotiate effectively over access fees. I will use Nasdaq's SuperMontage to illustrate my meaning.

Suppose a market order goes into SuperMontage, which then routes that order to another electronic communications network (ECN). (SuperMontage is now, in effect, an ECN.) Some ECNs charge an access fee of 3 mils per share, but others charge as much as 9 mils. If the order is being routed automatically to whichever ECN is displaying the best price, then the traders may be charged an access fee that they did not negotiate. This is not the way a competitive market should work. In a competitive market, buyers and sellers negotiate and arrive at a price that is mutually satisfactory. Even if they do not actually negotiate, the buyer can see the offered price and decide whether to accept it or find a more attractive price. That is how prices are set and adjusted in a competitive market, whether the market is for hogs or Nasdaq stocks. In the current market, however, if an order goes into SuperMontage and the trader does not specify handling rules to avoid the high access fees, the order can be assigned to an ECN that charges a 9 mil access fee, as opposed to another ECN that charges only 3 mils, which means that the trader generally cannot negotiate the exchange service fees.

Access fees, however, are necessary to allow an exchange to survive. Exchanges do not provide their services out of the goodness of their hearts. Running an exchange costs money, and the operators of the exchange are in the business to make a profit. A reasonable and competitive fee for services is appropriate.

But consider what happens in the markets. ECNs are charging traders 3 mils to obtain access for marketable orders. When the trade is done, they get 3 mils from the buyer of liquidity (the market order trader) and rebate 2 mils back to the seller of liquidity (the limit order trader or the standing quote). ECNs make their money on the difference. Instinet, SuperMontage, and Island all use this pricing system. Archipelago's system is similar, although not exactly the same.

But what is the actual price of exchange services? It is the difference between the access fee and the liquidity rebate, which is what the buyer and seller, acting collectively, pay to the exchange. Two prices are being quoted—the price for marketable orders and the price for limit or standing orders. The first one, the access fee, is a positive price; the second, the liquidity rebate, is a negative price. Separately, the two prices do not matter. Only the combination of the two matters.

How did this pricing system come about? ECNs assert that they are simply in the business of aggregating liquidity. According to them, they find the limit order traders that are willing to offer market liquidity by offering to pay them a 2 mil rebate if the order executes—an attractive offer for a limit order. ECNs do not want to foot the bill themselves, so they fund the rebates through the use of access fees. In turn, access fees come into play only when a market order is executed with the limit order, and those limit orders execute only when they become sufficiently stale that the other side of the trade is willing to pay 3 mils to reach the orders.

Each ECN has determined that it can do more business if it pays a little bit more for limit orders than its competitors. In this way, the ECN gets more orders, and it looks especially liquid and attractive. But suppose an ECN raises the liquidity rebate to 5 mils per share and finances it with an access fee of 6 mils. Most traders will not execute with those limit orders because they have to pay 6 mils to reach them. Those limit orders, therefore, will have to get even staler before they execute, which is not a particularly attractive situation. But traders' reluctance to pay these higher access fees will pass because the spreads will narrow. Most buyers and sellers do not notice mils when they trade, and few pay attention to the best representation of limit orders.

The concept of best execution normally pertains to market orders, although the mathematical methods for determining best execution apply equally to both limit and market orders. Soon enough, more traders will choose to do business with the ECN that offers a liquidity rebate of 5 mils per share, and soon after that, all the other ECNs will at least match that rebate because they must do so in order to be competitive. This is an agency problem between the broker, who is looking for the highest rebate, and the broker's client, who presumably is looking for the best execution. This situation promotes a system in which nothing determines the level of access fees and rebates separately. Only the difference between the two numbers matters, which means that the prices are indeterminate and no equilibrium exists.

One of many possible solutions would be to have a standard to ensure that when exchange services are priced, all interested parties understand the quote. If a quote is given at $20, the quote is $20—not $20 plus an access fee.

Consider a simple market composed of roughly equal numbers of buyers and sellers who are trying to solve similar trading problems and who can choose to use market orders or limit orders. If they all choose to issue market orders, no trades will occur.

If they all choose to issue limit orders, again, no trades will occur. Trading can occur only when the market contains both market orders and limit orders. What determines who will be a market order trader and who will be a limit order trader? Market orders offer fast execution. Limit orders presumably offer a wider spread. Spread is the price of liquidity. Thus, the spread balances the attractiveness of market orders and is the mechanism that encourages traders to participate with limit orders so that the market becomes symmetrical.

Into this simple environment comes a strange pricing rule that effectively says market orders will be taxed and the proceeds from that tax will be paid to limit order traders. The result is that spreads narrow. If spreads did not narrow, everybody would want to be a limit order trader, and once again, no one in the market would be able to trade. Spreads can narrow, but the end game remains the same; only the quoting of spreads changes.

Potential Solutions. Several solutions to this situation are available, including (1) net pricing, (2) passing fees through at confirmation, and (3) pricing standards.

■ *Net pricing*. If net pricing were applied, the exchange would include all fees and rebates (or whatever charges it establishes) in the quoted price. Thus, if a quote of $20 is standing and the fee for reaching that quote is nine-tenths of a cent, then the exchange would post the quote as $20 and 9 mils, or $20.009, not $20.

Unfortunately, if such net pricing were to be established, exchanges would have to move to subpenny pricing. This practice, however, would create such problems as penny jumping, with traders front running each other.

More fundamentally, two competitions take place in the same environment. The first competition occurs among the traders, who compete to find the best price. The buyer is looking for the lowest seller's price; the seller is looking for the highest buyer's price. This competition is typically priced in pennies, and many argue that it ought to be priced in nickels.

In addition to this first competition, a second competition occurs among exchanges, ECNs, and, in some cases, broker/dealers—in which markets compete to be the forum that hosts the first competition. This second competition is priced in mils, but it could be priced in sub-mils. For example, if the prevailing price were 1 mil, sub-mils would be used to beat the prevailing price.

Conducting both of these competitions on the same price grid is like mixing oranges and apples. It does not make sense to me.

■ *Pass fees through on confirmation*. Another possible solution is to pass the access fees through to customers on the trade confirmation sheet. This solution would likely be confusing and upsetting to investors and, thereby, might end access fee pricing. This solution, however, does not address the problems that arise when orders are unwittingly routed to ECNs with high access fees.

■ *Pricing standards*. A third possible solution is to create a pricing standard. This solution is not the same as setting a rate. All ECNs would set the access fee to zero and adjust their fees only on the liquidity side. This solution is sensible because the traders who submit the limit orders and the standing quotes are the people who have a relationship with the exchange. They can tell an exchange that its price is too high by doing business with another exchange. Conversely, they can tell an exchange that if it lowers its price, it will get more of their order flow. Market order traders do not have that liberty because they are seeking best execution anywhere they can find it.

Unfortunately, placing the entire exchange fee on standing limit orders and quotes may be politically difficult. The present pricing system appears to subsidize liquidity. This alternative would appear to tax liquidity. In practice, neither impression is true because limit order traders adjust their prices in response to the pricing before them so that the pricing convention does not matter. Perhaps a more politically feasible standard would be to split the fee between the buyer and the seller and allow only one-half to be adjustable and not the other.

A precedent exists for setting pricing standards. I believe that many states in the United States have a rule that requires businesses that advertise retail prices to advertise their credit price—the price charged when a credit card is used. Businesses can also announce that they will give discounts for payment in cash. They cannot, however, advertise the cash discount price and then impose a credit premium. Such an arrangement is simply a pricing standard. It does not set the price. The reason for the standard is obvious; it is in the consumer's interest that all advertised prices be on the same basis. The choice of the standard is less important than the imposition of the standard. In the credit card case, the particular standard chosen obviously reflects the interests of the credit card companies, which do not want customers to see the price of credit. A similar standard for exchanges would make all price quotes comparable.

Consider another analogy. Imagine two wholesale terminals in which vendors have stalls from which they sell apples. The apples sell for 20 cents per bushel net, but the two terminals have different pricing standards. Terminal A charges vendors 1 cent per bushel sold. As a consequence, the quoted price per bushel is 21 cents. Terminal B charges customers 1 cent per bushel bought, and as a consequence, the quoted price is 20 cents. Either way, the customer is going to pay 21 cents; either way, the vendor is going to receive 20 cents. No problem exists until the two terminals advertise the prices that their vendors are offering and customers see the apparent—but not real—difference.

Competition works best when prices are transparent and easily compared, which requires the implementation of common pricing standards. Competition also works best when agents and their principals decide who gets paid and who does the negotiating. Competition does not work well when a third party, an outsider, sets the price that market participants have to pay. For example, assume that a rule is established stating that the fee charged to the provider of liquidity must be the same as the fee charged to the user of liquidity, meaning that the access fee must be equal to the liquidity rebate. Several things might happen, none of which is good for competition. In one scenario, ECNs might begin specializing in serving only buyers or only sellers. In another scenario, ECNs might become linked with entities that can subsidize the ECN's liquidity providers through such back-channel methods as payments for order flow. This practice would, in turn, allow ECNs to charge high fees for certain orders, with the result that traders could be routed to high-fee orders without their consent.

Setting an access fee of zero would not allow ECNs that specialize only in order routing to make any money. This observation suggests that the fee problem is more complex than it might otherwise seem.

Recently, as I have considered the access fee problem, it has occurred to me that the market for exchange services actually consists of two markets, each of which should be separately priced. One market is for representation; the other is for order routing. The representation market, in which ECNs are like the stalls for the apple vendors, is the more costly market. It takes substantial resources to set up those stalls. The order-routing market is not nearly as expensive, although it certainly has its costs too. Despite the fact that these are two different service markets, many of our exchange systems bundle the two markets together, which creates the conditions for the access fee problem. The markets use the routing service to subsidize the order representation service, and they are getting away with it because of the agency problem associated with the submission of limit orders.

As I said earlier, competition works best when prices are transparent and easily compared. Only principals and their agents should decide who gets paid. These are the principles of good competition, and they need to be applied to access fees. But they should also be applied to other market inefficiencies, which I will discuss next.

Market Data Revenue

Market data revenues currently total about $400 million a year. These revenues are collected on a terminal-by-terminal basis and are then pooled, with the pools being distributed to the exchanges in proportion to the number of trades they do. The distribution system for these fees generates its own set of problems.

Problems. If a trader can control where an order goes, he or she has the power to influence the market data revenues that an exchange will receive. The exchanges, which are looking for these orders and are competing with each other, thus have begun to rebate the market data revenue to ECNs and, ultimately, to traders. Unfortunately, once exchanges begin rebating market data revenue, the process for making order-routing decisions becomes corrupted. Some brokers may stop making order-routing decisions based on best execution principles and look, instead, for side payments.

Such a corrupted process leads to other corruptions, such as tape shredding and wash trading. For example, assume that a trader has an order for 1,000 shares of stock and Island is displaying 1,000 such shares. The trader can submit the order and produce a single trade of 1,000 shares, or the trader can shred it into 10 orders of 100 shares each and pass them through the electronic pipeline. Because the system runs at very high speed, the trader can generally be assured of executing all 10 trades while receiving in return 10 times the anticipated market data rebate.

Besides tape shredding, wash trading to generate more market data revenue has occurred. This practice has elicited an SEC response that, in effect, cuts short a competitive market in the name of solving an enforcement problem, which I do not think is particularly good policy. But rather than criticize, I will offer what I believe to be more equitable and workable solutions.

Potential Solutions. One solution is to lower the data fees, an action that I am sure would be welcomed by the buy side. After all, the buy side believes it owns the data. The exchanges, of course, will argue that such a change would drive them out of business. But if going out of business were a real danger, the exchanges would simply raise the trading fees.

Consider another solution. Instead of distributing market data revenue based on the number of trades that are done in the market center, use the revenue to move participants closer to the market. Participants, however, are afraid of being pennied, front run, or quote matched—option extraction strategies for which they receive no compensation—if they get too close to the market. For example, assume that I put in an order to buy at $20. Because it is a large order, a smart trader knows that the order's execution will likely be flatfooted and slow. Therefore, that trader will cover my order with a buy order at $20 and a penny. A sell order arrives and executes at $20 and a penny, and the trader is in an attractive position. If the price subsequently rises, the trader makes money to the full extent of that price rise. If the price drops, the trader will simply sell to my order. The trader's potential return distribution on the upside is unbounded; on the downside, it is bounded at one penny.

This situation looks very much like trading an option. When I submitted my buy order, the smart trader grabbed a free option that I offered to the market for which I was not compensated. Thus, participants are reluctant to get too close to the market, even though it is in the public interest for them to approach the market. If participants are not compensated for the options they provide to others, they will offer fewer of them. But currently, they are giving away something valuable and are hurt by the practice. If the price runs up, their order will not be executed, and if the price drops, they will execute but wish they had not. This is a lose–lose situation that frustrates traders who would otherwise offer liquidity.

My recommendation, therefore, is to reward investors for making these options available. Remember, the reward is not the trade. The trade would only be a reward if a trade occurred every time liquidity was displayed. Because a trade does not occur every time, the reward must be for offering liquidity. Thus, instead of distributing market data fees according to the number of trades, I suggest distributing them according to the amount of time a participant is at the best bid or offer multiplied by the size being displayed. A pool would thus be created based on time multiplied by size displayed, totaled among all traders. Such a plan may sound complicated, but it is workable. Besides, it provides an incentive for participants to get close to the market. Furthermore, a second pool would be established for those who are exclusively at the best bid or offer; otherwise, everyone would just match the best bid or offer but no one would improve it. Then, to make everything work properly, a competitive rebate market would be needed to give traders the proper incentives from the exchanges that are receiving the rebates.

Establishing such a structure would create a tighter market, allow for more size to be displayed, provide a direct solution to the penny jumping problem, and increase the prospects for sensible entry, not subsidized entry.

VWAP

My final topic—and I will cover it briefly—is VWAP and its misuse as a benchmark.

The implicit assumption that motivates trader interest in VWAP is that if the price of a buy trade is lower than the VWAP, then the trade is a sound one. If the price of the buy trade is higher, then the trade is a poor one because it fails to match the benchmark. The attraction of VWAP is that it is an easy benchmark and reflects most investors' natural instinct to do no worse than average. Despite being riddled with shortfalls, VWAP remains extremely popular.

Other presentations in this proceedings have covered this topic, so I will discuss a slightly more subtle aspect of VWAP that has not yet been discussed.

Some dealers now offer VWAP orders. They offer to take their clients' orders at the beginning of the day and fill them at the VWAP determined at the end of the day, plus or minus some commission. Many clients find this offer attractive without realizing that the dealers can exploit the strategy. The clients end up diluting the value of their funds and cutting into their performance. I will tell you how this is done.

Dealers with these orders trade early in the day to accelerate the price impact of the order, pushing up the price for the remainder of the day. If subsequent prices stay above the dealers' VWAP, the market VWAP for the day will be above the dealers' VWAP—not a good execution for the order giver. With this type of execution, dealers do not fairly serve their clients. Customers will suffer from this inefficiency if they are not paying attention.

Conclusion

The current market structure suffers from several inefficiencies. Three important problems are market access fees, market data revenue, and the use of VWAP as a trading benchmark. If market participants become more aware of the effects of these factors on price transparency, best execution, and market competition, they may be able to effect change. I believe that ways exist to improve market efficiency, primarily through the use of pricing standards that would specify how prices are quoted without prescribing what those prices must be.

Question and Answer Session

Lawrence E. Harris

Question: How is the SEC's concern about access fees definitionally distinct from internalization or payment for order flow in dealer market structures?

Harris: Access fees are all about brokerage. Exchanges are in the exchange service business, as are brokers. They compete with each other. Access fees are essentially a commission. The liquidity rebate is payment for limit orders, which is a negative commission. The payment for order flow that we normally discuss is the payment by dealers to obtain market orders that they will fill. When brokers acting as agents for their clients route orders according to where they can obtain the greatest payments, whether those are limit orders or market orders, they may not be making the routing decisions at arm's length. Although there are arguments that suggest that the decisions are indeed being made at arm's length, the situation does not smell right. It looks like a kickback.

Internalization is a way of acquiring payment for order flow by proprietary traders, so it is essentially the same thing as the payment for order flow for market orders.

Question: Given the consolidation in the marketplace, particularly among ECNs of late, do you believe that the 3 mil access fee and 2 mil liquidity rebate are sustainable as a pricing model over the long term?

Harris: I don't see any process that could cause those numbers to drop. As long as there are a couple of ECNs competing for order flow, any ECN that lowers its liquidity rebate puts itself at a disadvantage. The only direction it can go is up. It has been stable for awhile, but that is largely because the SEC is concerned about the issue, and I don't think anybody wants to challenge the SEC on it.

Question: Has fragmentation increased in recent years? Do you see it as a problem?

Harris: I am not convinced that fragmentation is increasing. I think things are being brought together by information systems—and by arbitrageurs. Keeping a market together that has many different execution venues requires adequate information about quotes and adequate access to those quotes. If access is not available, then the system requires arbitrageurs who have access and information and who can put those two together. Such a distributed system entails costs for, among other things, maintaining the information resources, supporting the arbitrageurs, and operating the order-routing systems. The alternative to such a distribution system, however, is full consolidation, which can only be obtained by government fiat. Such an alternative would probably not be as responsive to demands for innovation in new technologies.

Those who want to see more consolidation typically say that they want to see more competition among traders looking for the best price. Those in favor of more diverse market structures typically want to see more competition in the exchange services.

To maximize the competition and make it most efficient among traders, consolidate the markets by fiat. To maximize the competition among people who provide exchange services, provide the freedom to fragment the order flow and then hope that enough good information is available to keep the system operating.

An additional cost of fragmented markets is the loss of a clean standard for best execution. In a fully consolidated market, at least for market orders among retail traders, best execution is simple: You obtain the best price, by definition, at the time the order executes because no other price is available.

Question: What do you think about QQQ (the Nasdaq 100 ETF) fund rebalancing trades when beating the closing price strategy is routinely used by the dealers, resulting in a significant market impact in the last 30 minutes?

Harris: I think that investment managers who are not careful about their transaction costs are not providing the best service possible for their investors. Managers who are willing to forgo alpha in favor of lower tracking error are acting in a manner inconsistent with the long-term interests of their investors. Investors, however, judge funds by how well they track because they want true index funds, so such shortsighted behavior is understandable. Fortunately, the money involved is not huge, but it is enough that people ought to be concerned.

Question: Can you comment on possible changes the SEC is considering regarding rules on IPO allocations and the associated conflicts of interest?

Harris: For a long time now, IPOs have been part of the hidden plumbing system on Wall Street. When I say hidden plumbing system, I'm talking about the means by which wealth travels from one party to another party in noncompetitive ways or in ways that are subject only to indirect competition that is not immediately priced. The pricing of IPOs creates situations in

©2003, AIMR®

www.aimrpubs.org • 65

which people can be rewarded for things that aren't necessarily being priced. This creates fantastic tools to exercise agency problems, and that is not good. The Commission is very concerned, and I expect there will be some sort of rule making on the issue.

The interesting question is whether, on any given issue, we should pursue enforcement strategies or structural strategies. I believe we should pursue enforcement strategies—private ones preferably, as long as they are cheaper than the alternatives. But at some point, the enforcement strategies become very expensive, and then it is sensible to pursue structural strategies. The danger of pursuing structural strategies is that you can get it wrong, and when you get it wrong, you compound the problem.

When pursuing structural strategies, I recommend telling people what they cannot do instead of telling them what they must do. In the first instance, if you make a mistake, people will find a way to bridge over the mistake because people can substitute very easily. When you tell people what they must do, however, they must do it, and if you have made a mistake, tremendous costs can be generated.

The notable recent exception is Regulation Fair Disclosure (FD), which closed another hidden plumbing system. In Regulation FD, we told people what they must do. We told people that if they chose to reveal information to one person, they had to reveal it to everybody. We did not tell them they had to reveal information to anybody, but once they revealed information to one person, they had to reveal that information to everybody. We did this to close off the hidden pipeline of insider trading. In my opinion, Regulation FD was a good idea, and the basis for it was so strong that it was sensible to tell people what they must do.

In general, I would like to see us telling people what should not be done rather than what should be done.

Question: Do you believe that the past private sector connections of the incoming senior staff could influence future SEC policy? If so, what sort of institutional safeguards could the Commission put in place?

Harris: One safeguard is to elect officials who will appoint people of integrity, discipline, and self-awareness and who can be fair and impartial judges on an array of issues. Furthermore, we should recognize that for the higher governmental appointments, the appointees should not be people who will want to advance their careers after their period of appointment. Ideally, we should avoid situations in which appointees could be thinking, "If I decide in this way, I may get that job after I am out of office. But if I decide the other way, nobody will give me the time of day."

Furthermore, it is essential that we expose all issues to the fullest and broadest debate possible. That is what the comment process and open meetings are all about. Another important part of the equation is the open and free media that we have in the United States. And ultimately, of course, the option exists for those who feel slighted to go to the U.S. Congress and express their opinion. By and large, I think the system works well. I believe it was Churchill who said that democracy is the worst political system save all the others. I agree with him.